THINKING ABOUT EDUCATION

Philosophical Issues and Perspectives

Edited by

Erskine S. Dottin
University of West Florida

Terry Armstrong
University of West Florida

Robert Cummins
University of West Florida

Patricia Edmisten
University of West Florida

David Fritz
University of West Florida

Erskine J. Ware
Pensacola Junior College

UNIVERSITY
PRESS OF
AMERICA

Lanham • New York • London

Copyright © 1990 by

University Press of America®, Inc.

4720 Boston Way
Lanham, MD 20706

3 Henrietta Street
London WC2E 8LU England

All rights reserved

Printed in the United States of America

British Cataloging in Publication Information Available

"The Value of Academic Freedom" copyright © 1989 by Thomas Auxter

"In the Eye of the Storm: Public Education's Struggle with
Alleged Secular Humanism in Mobile, Alabama—A Values Approach"
copyright © 1989 by Samuel M. Vinocur

"Recent Developments in Quantum Physics and Their Implications for
Philosophy of Education: Is There Conditional Determinism?"
copyright © 1989 by Donald L. Grigsby

Library of Congress Cataloging-in-Publication Data

Thinking about education : philosophical issues and perspectives /
edited by Erskine S. Dottin ... [et al.].
p.   cm.
"Papers ... presented during the 40th Annual Meeting of the Southeast
Philosophy of Education Society held at the University of West Florida,
Pensacola, Florida, March 5–6, 1988"—Pref.
Includes bibliographies.
1. Education—Congresses.   2. Education—Philosophy—Congresses.
I. Dottin, Erskine S.   II. Southeast Philosophy of Education Society.
Meeting (40th : 1988 : University of West Florida)
LB41.T44   1989   370'.1—dc20   89-33763 CIP

ISBN 0-8191-7504-8 (alk. paper)

The paper used in this publication meets the minimum requirements of American
National Standard for Information Sciences—Permanence of Paper for Printed
Library Materials, ANSI Z39.48-1984.

This book is dedicated to all those who, as the late Sir Winston Churchill once said, "... are willing to learn, but are not always willing to be taught."

TABLE OF CONTENTS

PREFACE vii

THE HOUSE OF INTELLECT: CORPORATE BASTION OR COLLEGIAL ACADEMY?

CHAPTER ONE 1

    The Value of Academic Freedom
    - Tom Auxter, University of Florida............ 1

    A Response to Tom Auxter: What John Dewey
    and Adam Smith Might Say to the University
    as Corporation
    - Joseph DeVitis, State University of New
    York, Binghamton 27

EDUCATIONAL REFLECTIONS AND PRAXIS

CHAPTER TWO 33

    Bertrand Russell and Some Thoughts on
    Education
    - Shirley Jespersen, University of
    Arkansas, Little Rock 33

    Learning to be Together: John Dewey's
    Theory of Experience, Group Dynamics and
    Experiential Education as Conceptual
    Foundations
    - Judy Vogt, University of West Florida 42

THINKING ABOUT EDUCATION

CHAPTER THREE 62

    The Very Idea of a Knowledge Base for
    Teaching
    - C.J.B. Macmillan, Florida State
    University 62

    Teacher Accountability for Student Learning
    - George Newsome, University of Georgia 70

    A Methodological Consideration in Socratic
    Dialogue
    - Richard J. Elliott and Patricia J.
    Austin, University of New Orleans 80

Teacher Subject Mastery Testing: A Partial
Alternative to Teacher Evaluation
- Carolyn Lavely and John Follman,
University of South Florida 89

THINKING ABOUT POLICY AND SOCIAL ISSUES

CHAPTER FOUR 107

Opacity as a Policy for Educational Policy
- Robert D. Heslep, University of Georgia ... 107

Comparative Perspectives on the American
Dropout Problem
- Richard Renner, University of Florida 116

In the Eye of the Storm: Public Education's
Struggle with Alleged Secular Humanism in
Mobile, Alabama - A Values Approach
- Samuel M. Vinocur, University of South
Alabama 130

PHILOSOPHICAL ISSUES AND PROBLEMS

CHAPTER FIVE 143

The New Moral Education and the Use of
Relativism: A Pragmatic Response
- Winston Bridges, University of South
Florida, St. Petersburg 143

Chance Metaphysics and Education
- Kenneth D. McCracken, University of
Tennessee, Martin 154

Recent Developments in Quantum Physics and
Their Implications for Philosophy of
Education: Is There Conditional Determinism?
- Donald L. Grigsby, University of Alabama,
Birmingham 159

RESEARCH IMPLICATIONS

CHAPTER SIX 166

There's a Pot 'A Brewin' in Psychological
Research Methodology: What Does it Mean
for Research in Education?
- Michael A. Orey, James W. Garrison, and
John K. Burton, Virginia Polytechnic
Institute and State University 166

Theoretic and Pragmatic Justifications For
Collaborative Research
- Jeffrey Roth
The University of Florida.................... 190

PREFACE

The papers in this volume were presented during the 40th annual meeting of the Southeast Philosophy of Education Society held at the University of West Florida, Pensacola, Florida, March 5-6, 1988. The intellectual diversity of the society is exemplified in the array of analytical approaches to thinking about education as captured in this volume.

The major priority in selecting papers for this volume was given to ideas that might facilitate the reader thinking about education from a philosophical perspective. Educational problems and issues may be examined and analyzed from different interpretive, normative, and critical perspectives. However, papers in this volume were selected in order to reflect (a) some of the on-going problems and issues in the educational domain, and (b) various modes of philosophical analyses.

If by definition critical thinking is "... the propensity and skill to engage in judicious reflective skepticism about any issue," then the papers in this volume should contribute to improving the study of education; not only for those with a philosophical disposition, but even for those who often are not stimulated to think about their own thinking, or to reflect upon their own reflecting.

The editors of this volume hope that its major contribution to the field of pedagogy might be in forcing persons to pull themselves back from the particulars of the educational enterprise, and to consider education and schooling in its entirety.

Chapter One

The Value of Academic Freedom

by

Thomas Auxter
University of Florida

The value of academic freedom can be determined in a number of ways. We can think about its value for individuals or for societies. We can think about the general welfare of humankind or about the life of the biosphere. We can look at academic freedom through God's eye or through the Devil's eye.

It is through the Devil's eye that society often views academic freedom. Indeed, there are powerful forces in society today that see the work of the Devil in much of the exercise of academic freedom -- both in the K-12 classroom and in higher education.

Instead of discussing academic freedom in abstract terms, I propose to discuss a recent series of attacks on academic freedom and to ask what value we are prepared to give to academic freedom after noticing how bad it would be if ongoing attacks in today's world were successful. This in turn helps us to decide what we might wish to do to preserve academic freedom.

While continuing assaults on basic freedoms should be a matter of concern in any event, there are reasons why we should be especially concerned today. In this decade there has been a disturbing trend in the United States -- a process of duplicating the very conditions that led to the rise of fascism in Germany. It is not necessary to have a conspiracy in order to duplicate these conditions, although a conspiracy of sorts is clearly in the making. Instead, what we must address is a trend toward establishing conditions -- in mass communications and in public education -- that lend themselves to the rise of fascism as evidenced by the case of Nazi Germany. The effect of these trends is to narrow the range of investigation and debate. A further effect is to put a damper on all social change except when it is in the direction of conformity to the national purpose and interest (as construed by those with a military-industrial agenda in hand).

It is not possible to discover the full value of academic freedom without asking about the value of intellectual freedom in society. Today we find that the intellectual freedom to inquire, express ideas and debate is being limited in strikingly similar ways in the spheres of communication and education. Since these trends occurred once before in our century, we should ask about the ultimate effects they have had on intellectual freedom in general and academic freedom in particular. Since these trends culminated in fascism, we should ask what formulations were given to intellectual and academic freedom at the time. How were these freedoms construed? What value was placed on them? This will clarify the nature of the choice before us today when we decide how much we value academic freedom.

I

In 1947 a Conference on Thought Control was held in Hollywood, with over six hundred artists and writers attending. They came to discuss what they could do about right-wing efforts to control what is expressed in films and the broadcast media. Politicians who identified themselves as "conservatives" wanted to make sure than nothing contrary to "Americanism" affects a mass audience. Members of the House UnAmerican Activities Committee were particularly upset by a line from a movie that referred to democracy as the idea that people share and share alike. The investigators saw this as evidence of communist infiltration into the media. Nevertheless, these investigators saw themselves as fair-minded public officials who allowed evidence to temper their judgements. For example, they dropped the belief that the pre-Shakespearean dramatist and poet, Christopher Marlowe, was a Communist when they found out how long he had been dead.

It is against this background that artists and writers gathered to talk about thought control in the media of mass communication. Leo Lania, a dramatist and journalist who had exposed fascist military rearmament plans in Germany in the twenties and was himself the target of persecution as a result of his reporting, was invited to speak. Lania called attention to an increasing tendency in U.S. newspapers to adopt a "way of reporting which reminds me of a very similar technique that was practiced by the few truly democratic papers in pre-Hitler Germany, when they gradually started to censor themselves of all news that might be objectionable to the growing forces of militarism and reaction."[1] He summarized what happened to German newspapers in the period before Hitler:

> It is simply not true that the Nazis had to come to power and turn their terror against the democratic press in order to make it conform to their wishes and orders. Long before, most of the liberal papers -- those with the largest circulation, like the papers of the Ulstein group -- gradually, and step by step, retreated and stopped printing the truth. They did not wait until they were confronted with strict censorship - they started to appease their future masters long before, so as to not be drowned in the mounting 'wave of the future.' Of course, they were drowned anyhow, in spite of their 'careful' and 'objective' treatment of controversial facts and events.

This is the process by which thought control was established in the media. The Nazis did not prevail due to superior intelligence, motivation or power. They would not have been able to gain power without "the defeatism and complacency of the liberals." Conformity to the national purpose (<u>Gleichschaltung</u>) "had already been accepted by the democratic German press, coerced into such a position by its financial backers, before it was ordered by Goebbels." This is the first lesson Lania draws from the German experience.

There are two other lessons he draws. One is that the "Nazis everywhere single out journalists [and] writers as their first targets." For the policy of <u>Gleichschaltung</u> to prevail Nazis must wipe out independent critical thinking. The targets are intellectuals of all kinds: "writers, journalists and artists" among others. These are the very people who have as their "most urgent and holiest mission" the task of making people think -- supporting them "with the tools they need in order to think freely and correctly."

The final lesson that Lania draws may be the most telling:

> For twenty years, in every European country, we have seen the Nazis conjure up a so-called Communist danger and, by presenting themselves as the saviors from danger, destroy the forces of democracy and progress.

These are the perennial "Red scares" which strike sympathetic chords in military and industrial circles.

The pattern of thought control outlined by Lania is clear enough. Control over mass communications begins with right-wing entrepreneurs buying up major portions of the media and trumpeting nationalistic causes and slogans. Even the more liberal and democratic news sources will fall under the influence of nationalistic sentiment if there is a sizeable right-wing movement ready to whip up patriotic fervor over every perceived threat to the nation and promote every conceivable extension of national hegemony and wealth. If we add to this mixture intimidation from right-wing forces determined to have the nation depicted favorably (in every respect and according to their specifications) and pressures from financial backers afraid their investments will be jeopardized in a rising tide of nationalistic feeling, the result will be obvious. The media will censor themselves -- gradually reducing coverage of events, issues, and points of view offensive to ardent nationalists. Ideas and interpretations not in keeping with the 'national purpose' will fade from view.

A series of "Red scares" accelerates the process of thought control. Nationalists claiming to save the country from communism can actually have the effect of dismantling democracy through the extravagant measures they propose for national security. In the either-or world of the right-wing imagination, anyone not supporting the national purpose, as conservatives define it (complete with a military and industrial agenda), is sympathetic to the enemy, as conservatives define it (complete with international conspiracies to impose a godless materialistic way of life on everyone). In such a world intellectuals and artists, groups known for more subtle interpretations of the world, are automatically suspect and are marginalized to the extent that they encourage independent critical thinking.

The danger of these patterns culminating in fascism is real. Lania's point is that these patterns are emerging in the United States. He is warning us to pay attention to where these trends lead and to notice the consequences of ignoring or underestimating the forces taking us in that direction. Lania knew where McCarthyism was headed -- even before Joseph McCarthy appeared on the scene to lead the charge.

Recent revelations about both McCarthy and one of his key supporters, Billy Graham, show how serious the threat really was and how successful mass communications can be in generating a Red scare. Only two years after Lania's warning, William Randolph Hearst and Henry Luce decided to use their vast powers over public consciousness (through their chains of newspapers and magazines) to create strong anti-communist feeling in the United States. The historical evidence on this development has been assembled by Ben Bagdikian, Dean of the Graduate School of Journalism at the University of California (Berkeley). In The Media Monopoly, Bagdikian informs us of the circumstances surrounding the decision by Hearst and Luce to choose Joseph McCarthy and Billy Graham as the standard-bearers for an anti-communist crusade that would be covered closely by media empires.

Billy Graham was virtually unknown at the time -- preaching to small audiences in a tent in Los Angeles. Bagdikian reports the results of the media attention:

> In late 1949 Hearst sent a telegram to all Hearst editors: 'Puff Graham.' The editors did -- in Hearst newspapers, magazines, movies, and newsreels. Within two months Graham was preaching to crowds of 350,000.[2]

A few weeks later Luce began puffing Graham as well. Graham himself now acknowledges the effect this had: "Time and Life began carrying about everything I did, it seemed like. They gave me a tremendous push."

Graham did not disappoint his media backers. He delivered lines like "Either Communism must die, or Christianity must die." Even worse, he publicly supported McCarthy and McCarthyism to the very end of the five-year state of siege in national politics.

New information on the relationship between McCarthy and Hearst reveals another dimension of the problem. Senator McCarthy was touring the country waving his famous list of communists he said had infiltrated the nerve centers of American life. In 1950 he used this tactic for the first time: "I have here in my hand a list of 205 names known to the Secretary of State as being members of the Communist Party...still shaping policy in the State Department." William Randolph Hearst, Jr., who was also a strong supporter of McCarthy at the time and who would later inherit the media chain, provides some telling evidence. "Joe gave me a call not long after that speech," Hearst said recently. "And you know what? He didn't have a damn thing on that list. Nothing." Nor was McCarthy ever able to turn up any communists in the half decade in which he helped to create a national trauma. Although media magnets knew this very well, they did not hesitate to publicize McCarthy's crusade without a hint of the true story. After all, it was their crusade, too.

Warnings issued by people like Lania were not heard amidst the rising clamor generated by the anticommunist crusade and amplified by media owners with an interest in the outcome. The sequence of events in the half decade of McCarthyism not only shows how easy it was to forge the links between right-wing political and religious personalities on the one hand and conservative owners of the press and airwaves on the other. With some knowledge of these patterns in the fifties, it is easier to appreciate Bagdikian's point about the damage that can be done when a handful of people gain substantial control of mass communications. This also makes the increasing threat of a media monopoly more troubling.

Bagdikian gives the statistical profile. Most of what is seen and heard, through all communications media, is now controlled by twenty-nine corporations, down from fifty only five years ago, down from hundreds only a few decades ago. Projections are that six corporations will soon control most newspapers, radio and television stations, magazines, and publishing houses. Of twenty-nine chief executive officers currently deciding what we find out, almost all have conservative political leanings.

The case studies discussed by Bagdikian reveal that those at the top are highly susceptible to financial pressures and are often willing to cooperate with conservative politicians in efforts to whip up public hysteria -- creating the nation's recurring Red scares and military preparations. Even worse, defense contractors like General Electric are buying up the media. The result of these factors coming into play at the same time is that we now have a media fixated on personalities as solutions to problems, obsessed with national defense issues, and reluctant to cover issues having to do with economic justice in the society.

If mass communication is the means by which people receive information about and interpretations of events, and if this is the basis for decisions about what people will or will not support, then limiting the scope and depth of what is communicated will affect the ability of citizens to question and oppose the goals of those with control over the media. If it also happens that those who exercise this control have politics to the right of center, then citizens will be less able to resist (in an informed way) the initiatives of those to the right of center. Reading Bagdikian's analysis against the background of Leo Lania's warnings gives us insight into where this trend leads. The tendencies we see in the ownership and operation of the sources of public information run parallel to the conditions that made way for a Hitler in the twenties and thirties.

II

If there is a trend limiting the access to and content of public education at the same time there are new limits on the coverage in mass communication, the result can be deadly. In education, as in communication, the parallel between what occurred in Germany and what is happening today in the United States is both striking and ominous. New limits on both the information citizens receive and on their ability to think about what that information means do not bode well for the future of democracy. At stake is the viability of independent critical judgement within the framework of democratic politics.

The erosion of academic freedom begins with political pressure building outside educational institutions -- pressure to make schools and colleges teach values supporting patriotic and religious priorities that a portion of society wants everyone to accept and promote (without exception and without qualification). Of course, it is not strictly necessary that patriotic and religious values be linked, but it does reinforce nationalistic tendencies if people become convinced that the nation-state is the protector of religious values they care about. A nationalistic movement becomes even more formidable if a sizeable minority believes the state is obligated to enforce a religious code the violation of which is an offense to God. In short, it is doubtful we will see a nationalistic juggernaut unless the nation becomes convinced that "God is on our side." The threat to democracy comes not only from sources that are authoritarian in nature; the sources are theocratic in nature as well.

The ultimate effect of this trend is to establish a standard by which all forms of expression are judged. Something akin to Goebbels conception of conformity to the national purpose is the final codified version of thought control defining the limits of inquiry and discourse. However, it is worth recalling the sequence of events noted by Lania: before there is an ultimate codification of what is permissible to express, before Gleichschaltung becomes the law of the land, right-wing forces will apply intimidation and financial pressure to create the same result, a kind of de facto conformity preceding de jure conformity. Alternating between cries about the danger of communism and condemnations of those who are soft on this "godless materialism," magnifying insults to national honor, using the media to push for "military preparedness," exalting masculinist "virtues" of fearlessness and aggression, insisting on a military and industrial agenda that will guarantee national superiority over all others, denying equality to women and to those who are ethnically "different," and demanding that we instill these values in our children are all prefigurations of the code of conformity. Ignoring or dismissing these prefigurations -- in effect, submitting to the intimidation -- hastens the ultimate codification and "the final solution."

A rising tide of nationalism affects more than just the perception of boundaries for the expression of thoughts and attitudes. Nationalism in its modern form, reinforced by a religious zeal for heaven and a worldly appetite for dominating trade, establishes a military and industrial agenda that affects in fundamental ways how education is structured and the extent to which education enables citizens to develop independent criticisms of the direction in which society is headed. An examination of the German model of disciplinary boundaries for higher education -- as that model took shape in the years before Hitler -- reveals ways in which nationalism can erode and consume the very institutions in society that are supposed to serve as critics of and guardians against the rise of mindlessness and fanaticism.

Konrad Jarausch traces developments in Germany that led to a replacement of a broadly-conceived liberal education, empowering citizens to criticize society, with a more technical education serving the interests of military and industrial sectors, fueling an intense and uncritical nationalism. Jarausch conducts an exceedingly careful multi-dimensional study of <u>Students, Society, and Politics in Imperial Germany</u>: <u>The Rise of Academic Illiberalism</u>.[3] It has the special advantage of giving the reader an eye onto the ways in which young people were socialized into a herd mentality and ultimately stampeded into a thundering herd called 'fascism.'

Jarausch analyzes several factors in higher education that collectively made it possible for an authoritarian personality to emerge and assume power without serious challenge. Among these factors are a nationalistic campaign directed at students, an increasing tendency (aggravated by periodic economic crises) to see higher education as a credentialing process for secure "professional" positions, constraints on both student and faculty activism, anti-Semitism on campus that was for the most part ignored by faculty, administrative efforts to suppress socialist ideas and organizations at the universities, and in the years of Hitler's ascendancy pressures to decrease student enrollment.

The path to fascism in Germany leads through a period of narrow research specialization and an unquestioning acceptance of the authority of the nation-state. All the while, German professors told themselves they were doing the right thing by advancing disciplinary research that in one way or another contributed to the power and status of an emerging industrial empire. It seemed inconceivable for them to criticize the state from the standpoint of their professional backgrounds because (a) disciplines were defined in ways that restricted professional achievement to relatively narrow research programs, and (b) they believed the contribution of a "good" professional was to pursue "pure" research, uncontaminated by "political" concerns which should be left to others to take up. They believed the best they could do was to remain strictly within lines of specialization and not comment on, much less work on, larger concerns. Only later did they discover that the road to fascism is paved with "good" professions.

The outlines and import of the proto-fascist model of higher education are now painfully clear. Under this conception academic freedom is the freedom of professionals to advance their own careers within disciplinary boundaries in those cases where that is compatible with state authority and the national purpose. It remains for us to examine what value is properly placed on academic freedom within a democratic society and to ask what significance recent trends in education, introduced under the banner of "the Reagan Revolution," have for the fateful choice between proto-fascist and proto-democratic models of higher education.

There are many ways to express the positive relationship between the value of academic freedom and other values accepted in a democratic and pluralistic society. It is obvious that for democracy to flourish it takes more than people voting on what they believe is in their interest. If people are not sufficiently educated (by whatever means) to exercise good judgement in the promotion of their best interests, democracy will not work very well. It will be a field day for right-wing politicians claiming to represent the interest of the people, through nationalistic and materialistic ventures, while actually promoting interests in society that degrade the environment and waste resources on weapon systems that destabilize the world situation and threaten peace. If people are not educated well enough to vote for their long-term interests, which will include the health of their children in a sustainable world, then they will accept offers of short-term material benefits (more jobs, a boost to the local economy, etc.) that will ultimately bring harm to them.

It may be that there are some societies that function well enough, in terms of sharing information, openly discussing what is happening, and facing few external threats so that institutions of higher education are not crucial to the formation of balanced judgements about current economic and military proposals in relation to the anticipated consequences. As it happens, there are few such societies left on Earth. For the foreseeable future, higher education will have the essential role of cultivating independent judgement for a sustainable economy, for a viable democratic politics and for world peace. In our situation we need more than technical judgements about whether some specialized project is workable on its own terms. We need to think about, and make judgements about, how various projects go together and what consequences will emerge from our choices.

The extreme orientation toward careers and making money in today's society, with extreme consequences for what is offered as education, makes it hard to believe that education has often been a very different kind of activity. In the western world there have been academies, from the earliest times, dedicated to the Greek ideal of character formation and human excellence (arete). The goal for the cultivation of judgement is the ability to temper one's judgements (sophrosyne), always seeking relevant evidence. With this conception, education becomes a many-sided process of development, cultivating the many sides of human beings so that they can appreciate considerations that have a bearing on fundamental choices as well as on immediate practical decisions. The goal of this educational process is directly at odds with the goal of restricting education to vocational and technical preparation. It is in the interest of people who prefer democracy to choose the more traditional educational ideal over the ideal that has prevailed recently in a period distinctly more materialistic and nationalistic than others.

Before examining the bill of particulars for education submitted by the Reagan Administration, it will be helpful to look at the general trends of the patterns in the United States in the eighties. These assessments of general trends will enable us to see how the Reagan-era proposals affect the nature and direction of recent developments.

Three recent, widely discussed reports have urged major reforms in undergraduate education. The Education Commission of the States, the National Governor's Association, and the Carnegie Commission issued separate studies criticizing the content, teaching methods, and administration of programs leading to the baccalaureate degree. The reports share concerns about access to higher education, poor advising, decision making by administrators who are isolated from faculty and students, and lack of rewards for good teaching.

The Carnegie report, <u>College: The Undergraduate Experience in America</u>, is at once the most critical and the most hopeful. The main criticism is that the specialization of knowledge, combined with the vocational orientation of today's student, create college graduates who are narrow in outlook and willing to defer to experts on issues that call for judgements from educated citizens. There is a "decline in public understanding" of issues at a time when both the fate of democracy and the survival of the planet depend on recognizing human interdependence.

Universities come in for especially severe criticism. The reward system at universities is geared toward research. While it is understandable that centers of research will seek to reward research, this priority overshadows everything else. Hence, faculty quickly get the message that good teaching counts for little; universities value quantities of publications.

The report paints a bleak picture of undergraduate education at universities. The Carnegie survey shows that while students choose education to promote career goals, they respond (almost) as strongly to "becoming well-rounded," "developing talents and abilities to the fullest," and "learning more about things of interest."

But when the Carnegie research team visited campuses, it did not often find undergraduates motivated toward this kind of development. Specialization and fragmentation of knowledge have occurred to such an extent that when researchers take time out to teach, which is not rewarded, they tend to dwell on their research interests, which are rewarded.

Undergraduates record the information they need to cover the specialization. The goals of educating the student to inquire and to form independent judgements slip away in the effort to impart the latest knowledge on specialized topics.

The Commission's criticisms can be summarized as follows:

> For those who care about government "by the people," the decline in public understanding cannot go unchallenged. In a world where human survival is at stake, ignorance is not an acceptable alternative. The full control of policy by specialists with limited perspective is not tolerable. Unless we find better ways to educate ourselves, as citizens, unless hard questions are asked and satisfactory answers are offered, we run the risk of making critical decisions, not on the basis of what we know, but on the basis of blind faith in one or another set of professed experts.[4]

Yet the Carnegie survey also shows that faculty <u>like</u> to teach and would put more into it, if they were not punished (in a professional sense) for doing so. The report recommends revising the reward structure, in several ways, so that teaching is valued. This includes establishing faculty positions for Distinguished Teaching Professors. It also includes developing the model of the "scholar-teacher." The idea is to increase the importance of the teaching done, not to increase the teaching load.

The report recommends curriculum reform in general education and in the approach to major disciplines. "We found that narrowly focused courses in English, science, and history often were easily relabelled general education."

The Carnegie Commission calls for courses that feature themes connecting the disciplines and showing the relevance of various types of knowledge to central questions -- with heavy emphasis on students coming up with the answers. General education should extend throughout the undergraduate years, not serve as a hurdle at the beginning. Moreover, departments should offer "enriched majors" that "help students put their field of study in perspective." The report sees hopeful signs: several colleges and universities are already putting these ideas into effect.

Perhaps the most important aspect of the Carnegie Commission report is that it highlights the danger to democracy of the strictly disciplinary approach to higher education. Coming at the end of a decade of educational "reform" promoted by the Reagan Administration, it serves as a warning of where the conservative model of education leads -- even though the specific initiatives of the Reagan era are not the subject of the report and are not discussed in it.

Within a conceptual framework that links the values of education and democracy, and against the background of an historical example of a model of higher education that lends itself to the rise of fascism, the significance of the Reagan Revolution becomes clear. In order to appreciate this point, it is necessary to consider the goals and policies of the Reagan Administration as a whole, as a series of actions having a cumulative effect.

Consider the following: (1) A major shift of federal resources -- away from education (including scholarships) and towards the military -- occurred within the first months of the Reagan Administration. The Secretary of Education, William Bennett, announced he was against the very existence of a Department of Education, but inasmuch as he was the Secretary of it, he would do his best to cut the budget and dismantle federal programs. (2) Research programs funded by the military replace other types of basic research in science, and the strict peer-review process is waved in favor of military review and approval of projects. (3) The new administration pushes vouchers for private schools -- promoting religious education at the expense of public education. (4) William Bennett and Phyllis Schlafley draft new regulations for implementation of the Hatch Act (which had merely prohibited psychological testing of students without a parent's permission). They interpret it to mean that there can be no discussion of values in the classroom and devise a reporting form (distributed by Schlafley's Eagle Forum) so that parents can report to the federal government any teacher discussing values. (5) Major restrictions on access to government information are introduced, and federal agents report on who is using libraries. (6) The Reagan

Administration announces it will be aggressively promoting the development of research parks so that educational resources can be applied (diverted) to building up the industrial strength of the nation.

An orientation toward economic power designed to support the nation-state results in a contradiction between the pretension of supporting life and the result of destroying life. Ironically, in both Germany and the United States the protofascist forces take it as an article of faith that abortion is always wrong and consequently present themselves as "pro-life," masking the overall effect of an approach to life that is manifestly and essentially pro-death. This orientation is evident in the rush to adopt increasingly destructive weapon systems -- sacrificing everything developmental in life for the sake of evermore awesome implements of death. It is also evident in the rush to accumulate wealth for the nation-state and its citizens -- accepting any form of environmental degradation (especially if it can be dumped on the Third World) for the sake of building up the infrastructure of an industrial empire.

The effect on academic life of permitting the military to dictate research priorities and programs is examined by Ira Winn in the "The University and the Strategic Defense Initiative."[5] Professor Winn takes note of some recent comparisons drawn between patterns in Germany earlier and trends in the United States today. Winn also notices that the decision university faculty and staff have to make on whether to accept "cornucopias of lucrative (SDI) research contracts" has a lot to do with whether we wish to follow the German path. Indenturing university research to military agendas limits the ability of faculty to perform the function of criticizing society. It creates incentives to follow the path of authority, which is also where the money leads. Disciplinary research, narrowly conceived and designed to satisfy military and industrial requirements, is not conducive to questioning the priorities of the military-industrial complex.

Winn makes it clear enough how this happens with military contracts. It remains to be seen how research parks linking universities to industry, can also have the effect of quieting faculty.

III

The transformation of human life into the image of a corporation is a specter hard to ignore in the modern world. The corporate model has increasingly become the basis for social organization and estimations of individual worth at all levels in the United States. This has not happened by accident. For the past decade we have had a national administration dedicated to the task.

A 1984 interview with D. Bruce Merrifield, Assistant Secretary of Commerce, provides insight into the mentality seeking to reduce everything to the value of money derived from corporate competition in world markets:

> We have the best capital development capability, the world's largest market, and a unique entrepreneurial culture. We have all the elements needed--*if* we just remove the barriers to collaborative efforts that are necessary for world competitiveness.[6]

According to Merrifield, we must harness intellectual energy in research and development programs so that "we can outrun anybody, anytime, anyplace." He concludes that the research park, in which university developed research is transferred to the private sector, is the key to corporate success.

Notice the euphemism for controlling how intellectuals will use their minds: "removing the barriers to collaborative efforts." Penetrating and organizing all of life for the sake of private profit is called "world competitiveness." Taking away resources for independent research is "capital development capability."

In "The Marriage of Alma Mater to Adam Smith" John Buescher examines the tensions and conflicts introduced into academic life when universities become intimately involved with corporations in setting up research parks. He notes several ways that collaboration for the aggressive pursuit of wealth -- the promotion of what Merrifield would call "capital development capability -- distorts and corrupts academic values. Buescher argues that inducing faculty and students to complete

16

the many routine tasks required to make profits would divert them from theoretical inquiry that would ultimately help them to become more innovative researchers. The bitter irony is that while essential academic values are sacrificed for the dream of wealth, the long-term effect is not even to produce the greater "world competitiveness" people like Merrifield are seeking.[7]

The meaning of the corporate model for higher education was recently brought home to faculty at the University of Florida in a series of incidents which at first seemed unrelated. The real story started when the University announced plans for a research park -- on the Reagan Administration model. The park, called "Progress Center," is located several miles from campus and emphasizes biotechnology. The anticipated growth in the area whetted the appetites of Florida's entrepreneurs and developers.

But there was a problem. The research park is situated in a relatively undeveloped "recharge" area that drains into the Florida Aquifer, a source of much of the state's fresh water. Some faculty members, including a respected scientist who chaired the Sierra Club, argued at public hearings that it would be a serious mistake to place a biotechnology research park, which uses toxic chemicals, in this sensitive area where accidents could poison the drinking water and damage the ecosystem. The faculty were convinced they had contributed their expertise to the public interest and to the local community.

The Chamber of Commerce, however, saw things differently. On a tape of a Chamber executive committee meeting that was leaked to the press,[8] the Chamber president boasted about promises he had just won from the university president to subdue faculty expressing opposition to economic development. Specifically, the university president "committed to this, among other things: that every time a member of his faculty gets up at a public meeting or writes a letter that is dilatory about economic development or about this community, he will get someone of equal or higher credentials to write a letter or go to a public meeting in opposition to that point of view." Added the Chamber president, "That has a chilling effect on future letters."

The Chamber president became even more specific about the commitment of the university president: he wants to know the times faculty speak at public meetings so that he can determine if they have neglected duties at the university. "He wants to know that. I mean, I didn't generate that, he asked that question."

As the Chamber president was spelling out this new set of commitments, other members of the executive committee made comments like, "Oh, outstanding" and "Oh, this is super." At one point the Chamber president responded to a member of the committee, "Your side is really bubbling, lady," evoking a reply, "Sounds like fun."

Before reporters published the tapes, they asked the Chamber president whether these commitments had actually been made. Twice he told them that they had. But when the story hit the newspapers, the Chamber president immediately resigned and said that he had "embellished" the truth in the course of a meeting that was "upbeat" and "motivational." The student newspaper, in an editorial entitled, "Chamber of Horrors," wrote pointedly, "It is horrible to think they include restricting free speech among the upbeat things in life."

The university president immediately issued a brief statement asserting that "faculty have the right to express themselves as individuals." He interpreted this as the "true expression of any individual's sincere feeling," insofar as that is protected by the First Amendment. This definition made faculty somewhat uneasy since the real issue had to do with the expression of their professional judgements as members of the university community.

A week later the university president explained his position to the faculty senate. He passed quickly from remarks on "alleged abridgements to academic freedom" to his point: "if the University and the community cooperate and grow together, each will nourish and improve the other." He emphasized that the community would have to abandon its "no-growth mode" if the University is to achieve its full potential as a "world class educational institution." The only obstacle to greatness, he said, is "our apparent inability to pull together," symbolized by "a vocal minority of dissenters." It is not enough to protect dissent: "dissent from the dissenters should be protected and encouraged." In closing he stressed that "we must grow together" and that "partnerships with private enterprise are the hallmark of a successful teaching and research university."[9]

The same week, United Faculty of Florida (NEA), the bargaining agent at the campus, demanded an investigation in a joint news conference with the Sierra Club, the Audubon Society, and the American Civil Liberties Union. The chancellor of the state university system sent two representatives to investigate. After a five-hour visit, and without talking to faculty targeted for "the chill," the investigators issued a news release: the university president was innocent of all charges and a "victim" of bad publicity.

Once "the chill" became a focus of attention, earlier events took on a new meaning. About six months before the Chamber meeting, the university administration had placed the philosophy department in "receivership" and threatened it with abolition.

The philosophy department had been a longtime source of campus activism and dissent, most recently a center of organizing efforts to get the university to divest from South Africa and cut ties with corporations that do business there. One of those same corporations was potentially a client for the research park.

The fact that most philosophy classes closed out did not impress administrators; nor were they impressed with teaching evaluations among the highest in the university. Administrators complained about insufficient grants and "national visibility" and were bothered by "a lack of collegiality."

In a deposition given in response to a lawsuit filed over the threat to the department, the university president presented his conception of how the university is organized and how this is related to the possible abolition of philosophy: "Well, first of all, the Vice President for Academic Affairs is the chief academic officer of the university. He has direct supervisory responsibility of the deans of the colleges who are in effect managers, the academic managers, of the colleges." Question: "Is abolition of the department still a possibility?" Answer: "Abolition of any department of the university would always be a possibility if we're not doing the job we're sent here to do." Other administrators testified that philosophy is not as "productive" as other units.

Finally, local newspapers have recently published information that may explain the university's reluctance to move the site of the proposed research park and the need to quiet professors. An officer of the university foundation that oversees development of the research park formed an investor group that bought land adjacent to the park for a real estate development.

This raised questions about what other land in the area had been slated for development and who will profit from these ventures. Requests for full financial disclosure have gone unanswered, and opposition continues.

The Florida experience shows that the price paid for the university-business "collaboration" proposed by the Reagan Administration can be even higher than the diversion of teaching and research energies into more "productive" ventures enhancing "capital development capability." We may also have to sacrifice the faculty expertise that would otherwise be devoted to the public interest and perhaps even the programs populated by faculty and students inclined toward activism and dissent.

We are getting close to the bottom line for the university-as-corporation. Once we get there, we may or may not have faculty left who will ask the question, "Is there academic freedom after research parks?" On the balance sheet of profits and losses of the university-as-corporation, will the comptroller even notice that academic freedom is missing?[10]

IV

To what extent do faculty members today believe that there is a serious threat to academic freedom? To what extent would faculty commit themselves to a defense of the value of academic freedom if they had a full picture of the many ways it is in jeopardy? To what extent are they currently organizing to do something about it?

The 1988 Conference on Academic Freedom, co-sponsored by the National Education Association and the University of Florida Holland Law Center, gives us the beginnings of answers to these questions.

The keynote speaker for the first night of the conference was NEA Vice President Keith Geiger, who described what the organization that represents two million educators is prepared to do in order to meet recent threats to academic freedom. Geiger emphasized that the nature of threats to academic freedom has changed in recent years.

Earlier in the century educators assumed that faculty and administrators would stand united in the defense of academic freedom. It was expected that threats would come from outside the campus. Some of the most eloquent statements on academic freedom were made by administrators.

But in today's world we find "the triumph of an entrepreneurial mind-set within the academy." Geiger noted that the vocabulary of higher education has become saturated with the "language of commerce." "Today we are told with increasing regularity that knowledge is a commodity, education an industry, learning an asset, research an enterprise. And always and everywhere, there buzzes loudly the buzz-word competitiveness. Obviously, it is now a given that the purpose of education is to ensure that Fords and Chryslers outsell Toyotas and Nissans."

Geiger cited the dissenting opinion given by Justice William Brennan in the Yeshiva case as an accurate summary of "the erosion of the faculty's role in institutional decision-making": "Education has become 'big business' and the task of operating the university enterprise has become transferred from the faculty to an autonomous administration, which faces the same pressures to cut costs and to increase efficiencies that confront any large industrial organization."

This explains why part-time faculty have proliferated, now holding over forty percent of faculty positions. Today's administrator is seeing an advantage in having a faculty that requires no expensive fringe benefits and no rights of due process that restrict what administrators do with their power. "Part-timers become the pawns of those whose interest is in cost-effectiveness rather than educational excellence."

What can faculty do to turn the tide against "those who believe that the business of education is business?" Geiger asks educators at all levels to join the efforts of the National Education Association in defeating "the threats to academic freedom that today shame our nation." "We have the clout, the resources, the experience, the apparatus. We have influence in Congress, in state legislatures, in local government. We know labor relations. We know how to negotiate. And we know how to use the courts. Preserving academic freedom, strengthening faculty autonomy, and ensuring faculty dignity will require all of this and more."

James Davenport, President of the National Council for Higher Education, pointed to a series of recent court decisions that both reveal the agenda of "the repressive forces of the far right" and show why educators should unite to defend academic freedom. These cases -- dealing with issues ranging from textbook banning to the teaching of creation science to the purging of "secular humanism" from the classroom -- have often stemmed from conflicts at the K-12 level but established precedents for all levels of education. This should bring us to the realization that "the successful defense of any educator's rights is a victory for all educators."

"Academic freedom is under assault. It is now clear that if faculty, as employees and professionals, intend to protect themselves from victimization and reclaim integrity for their profession, they must acknowledge that they are participants in a struggle that is through and through political. And they must acquire the skills to work effectively within highly politicized settings." It will take an organized faculty to save academic freedom from the assaults that are "greater in force and greater in number than at any time since the McCarthy era."

Plenary speaker Ellen Schrecker made it clear that the pattern during the McCarthy period was anything but an organized response on the part of the faculty. In "McCarthyism and Academic Freedom: What Can We Learn?" she takes note of a peculiar phenomenon: "the almost complete lack of collective action by university faculties in support of their colleagues' political rights." Those who were attacked were regarded as having suffered individual misfortunes which they might have avoided if they had been more cautious. The response was for everyone to become more cautious. She develops an analysis of this history in <u>No Ivory Tower: McCarthyism and the Universities</u>.[11]

"Today, the narrowing of academic freedom is part of a much, much broader campaign which has under the Reagan Administration moved American political discourse far to the right and is seeking -- as it did during the McCarthy period -- to delegitimize whole areas of social and political concern. Given this situation, we can no longer afford to treat individual academic freedom cases as individual cases." She concludes that "recognizing the political nature of academic freedom violations and developing a collective response to them is the academic equivalent of obtaining a Major Medical Plan."

Fletcher Baldwin (Holland Law Center, University of Florida) looked at recent Supreme Court decisions concerning First Amendment rights. In general the Supreme Court has avoided defining academic freedom. The Court has been reluctant to get into this issue and has deferred to what administrators or collective bargaining contracts call for in a situation. In today's context, with over half of the lower court appointees made by the Reagan Administration, it is unrealistic to expect a remedy for academic freedom violations from the courts -- unless faculty have a collective bargaining contract to back them up in their complaints.

Julius Getman, President of the American Association of University Professors, observed that most of today's violations of academic freedom come from cases in which the "religious right" is promoting "efforts to impose an orthodoxy wherever they have the power to do that" and from "problems with sponsored research," when the military or industry attempts to exert control. Curiously, in the eighties attacks on academic freedom are usually made in the name of excellence, Getman noted.

Leonard Minsky, President of the National Coalition for Universities in the Public Interest, a Ralph Nader group supporting litigation in academic freedom cases, spoke about threats that are coming from the military and from industry. The money is flowing, he said, from these sources to the universities. Whether it is SDI or research parks that draw commitments of faculty time and energy, the result is that higher education is transformed. The bottom line becomes the new standard governing higher education. If the program doesn't pay off at the bottom line, administrators contemplate getting rid of the entire program -- eliminating tenured faculty in the process. In each of the academic freedom cases the Coalition has supported, the main factors behind the violations have been some combination of expecting financial advantage and an "ideological motive."

Conference organizer Hernan Vera commented that the sessions generated a great deal of energy on all levels. A Congressional hearing on academic freedom is now in the making. At the local level community groups are asking for a follow-up conference on universities and the public interest. A newsletter will be established; an academic freedom archive will collect material on cases around the country; and a proceedings volume from the conference will appear shortly. Perhaps most important of all, representatives from the various national organizations concerned with academic freedom issues agreed that they should be working together more closely and sharing information on developments and trends.

This conference marked a turning point that can only be appreciated by comparing it with the Conference on Thought Control held four decades ago. Both conferences were held in response to a wave of right-wing attacks on freedom of expression. Both brought together representatives of organizations defending intellectual freedom and professionals who would be affected by new limits imposed on inquiry and expression. Both were oriented toward mapping out strategies for defending the freedom necessary for a diverse and challenging intellectual and artistic life.

But the earlier conference generated little more than a short-term partisan effort to elect Progressive Party candidates in 1948. There was not an organizational basis for resistance to repression left in place when the Progressive Party was defeated. What followed was McCarthyism.

The 1988 conference was formed to look at recent threats with an eye toward providing the organizational support needed for an effective defense of academic freedom. This conference closed with a plenary session on "The Future of Academic Freedom," forging a consensus on specific proposals for coordinating the efforts of all who wish to defend intellectual life against the new wave of attacks.

Participants at this conference were aware of the need to avoid the mistakes intellectuals made during the McCarthy period. Speakers were emphatic about seeing an attack on academic freedom as more than the problem of the individual immediately affected. Several spoke about something tantamount to a moral obligation in today's context to support organizations defending educators under attack.

Individuals standing by themselves appealing for help from other individuals will not defend themselves successfully. Without organized resistance to the right-wing forces intent on introducing into education (at all levels) their agenda of strict conformity, academic freedom will be lost. If this comes to pass, it will mean that intellectuals were not intelligent enough to learn from the last serious brush with fascism, namely McCarthyism, that they must organize themselves or be prepared to give up the freedom of inquiry and expression they have taken for granted as a condition of life.

Although right-wing attacks on academic freedom subsided for two decades, they have picked up again -- this time with a ferocity, single-mindedness, and power of coordination that makes the threat even more real. That is one crucial difference in the situation today. Another is that we now have an organizational basis for defending educators against these attacks. Indeed, organizations of educators that have always thought of themselves as competitors are now cooperating on academic freedom issues. Consequently, though the threat is more real, the possibility of an organized response is also more real. It remains to be seen whether faculty in higher education, historically a group that has regarded itself as comprised of individuals dedicating critical intelligence to individual projects, will organize seriously to provide the "critical mass" necessary to protect academic freedom.

NOTES

1. Howard Koch, ed., Conference on Thought Control (Beverly Hills, CA., 1947).

2. Ben H. Bagdikian, The Media Monopoly (Boston: Beacon Press, 1987).

3. Konrad H. Jarausch, Students, Society, and Politics in Imperial Germany (Princeton, N.J.: Princeton University Press, 1982).

4. Ernest L. Boyer, College: The Undergraduate Experience in America (New York: Harper and Row, 1987), pp. 279-80.

5. Ira Winn, "The University and the Strategic Defense Initiative," Thought and Action, Fall 1987, pp. 19-32.

6. D. Bruce Merrifield, "Not an Adversarial Relationship" Thought and Action, Fall 1984, pp. 83-96.

7. John Buescher, "The Marriage of Alma Mater to Adam Smith" Thought and Action, Fall 1987, pp. 33-50.

8. The Gainesville Sun, February 17, 1987.

9. The University President, who resigned in 1989, is a former Florida Council of 100 (a business lobby) president and a lawyer specializing in corporate law.

10. Earlier versions of portions of sections III and IV appeared in Thought and Action (Spring 1988) and Florida Higher Education Bulletin (January 1987 and March 1988) under the titles "The Bottom Line for the University-as-Corporation," "Reports Urge Major Reforms in Undergraduate Education," and "Recent Threats to Academic Freedom" respectively.

11. Ellen Schrecker, No Ivory Tower: McCarthyism and the Universities (Oxford: Oxford University Press, 1986).

CHAPTER ONE

A RESPONSE TO THOMAS AUXTER: WHAT JOHN DEWEY AND ADAM SMITH MIGHT SAY TO THE UNIVERSITY AS CORPORATION

by

Joseph L. DeVitis
S. U. N. Y. Binghamton

I thank Tom Auxter for alerting us to the peculiar bedroom arrangement which occurs when academia appears to "jettison its unique obligations and responsibilities to [students, scholars, and society] in a rush to embrace narrowly defined industrial interests."[1] Classic cases in the history of assaults on academic freedom in American higher education should have been sufficient to make us aware of the oftentimes curious--and sometimes egregious--nexus between industry and education. In looking back to 1900, we recall the infamous case of E. A. Ross' dismissal from Leland Stanford University. That case was investigated by a committee of the American Economic Association, which published a scathing report showing that the dismissal was largely due to Ross' views on silver and municipal ownership--views which ran counter to those of one Mrs. Leland Stanford. Professor George E. Howard, another Stanford economist of the time, discussed the Ross case in bold fashion: "I do not worship Saint Market Street; I do not reverence Holy Standard Oil; nor do I doff my hat to the celestial Six Companies."[2] Professor Howard was required by Mrs. Stanford to make public apology or resign. Very courageously, Professor Howard resigned.

You will obviously note some parallels to the Ross-Howard case in the scenario outlined in Professor Auxter's paper, especially the examples of the president of the Chamber of Commerce in Gainesville and his apparent alter-ego at the university across town. Fortunately, neither proved to be as powerful as Mrs. Leland Stanford. However, their efforts should remind us that we need to be as vigilant today as Professors Ross and Howard had been in 1900. Indeed, we may well need to be more vigilant.

In line with the "stranger than fiction" (but unfortunately real) scenario offered by Tom Auxter, I propose two illustrious, if curious bedfellows in academe's history to help lead us out of the Florida twilight zone to some firmer foundations by which to judge connections between industry and education. My curious candidates, John Dewey and Adam Smith, doubtless would not have enjoyed each other's company; but their normally divergent streams of thought can ironically assist us in the matter at hand.

In his classic paper on "Academic Freedom" (1902) Dewey drives home the point that I wish to emphasize from the outset; for the battle enjoined by Professor Auxter and his dissenting colleagues is one we all share, no matter where we ply our professional trade: "Whatever wounds the body of truth in one of its members attacks the whole organism."[3] Dewey enlarges upon this "truth-function" premise in a manner that bears directly on the wider issues at stake in the University of Florida research park and philosophy department episodes: "Any attack, or even any restriction, upon academic freedom is directed against the university itself. To investigate truth; critically to verify fact; to reach conclusions by means of the best methods at command, untrammeled by external fear or favor, to communicate this truth to the student; to interpret to him its bearing on the questions he will have to face in life--this is precisely the aim and object of the university. To aim a blow at any one of these operations is to deal a vital wound to the university itself."[4]

It takes no academic Sherlock Holmes or Pinkerton man to direct us to where Dewey would aim his laurels, bows, and arrows in the case in hand. Unlike Mrs. Leland Stanford or the president of the University of Florida, Dewey would be forthrightly defending the more powerless philosophers across the quadrangle who seem to be doing and practicing what he would suggest are the inherent and essential truth-functions, in both aim and method, of any decent university community of scholars. Like Professor Howard in the Stanford case, Auxter and his dissenting colleagues need not apologize or retreat. Parenthetically, the president of the Chamber of Commerce in Gainesville has already retreated, however unwillingly; and his resignation might be interpreted as a partial apology for his ill-conceived efforts. Evidently, the same can still not be said for the university president across town. His tactics would doubtless draw Dewey's wrath even more, for several obvious reasons: (1) a university president should know better; and (2) as a university president, he is duly delegated to protect the ultimate goals and methods of the university community, i.e., its concerns for traditions of transmission of truth and the discovery of truth, wherever it may lead.

According to Dewey, these functions are necessary and neither can ever be entirely absent from the inner-and-outer-workings of the university community. He would further contend that _local_ and _temporal_ considerations do influence the exact ratio by which the truth function of the university is actually practiced. On Dewey's terms, then, the president of the University of Florida has not displayed substantial concern for the inherent and essential goals of the university; nor has he engendered and encouraged fertile ground for their discovery. Quite the opposite. Consequently, he has produced a really curious commodity: apparent failure on those very _local_ and _temporal_ grounds upon which he had hoped to "strike oil," as it were, for his university.

Furthermore, the president of the University of Florida has done some other very un-Deweyan things for the professor's wider view of the concept of freedom of work. For Dewey, freedom of work is even more fundamental than the academic freedom to express opinion. This is the case because, in Dewey's words, freedom of work "is an intangible, undefinable affair-something which is in the atmosphere and operate as a continuous and unconscious stimulus. It affects the spirit in which the university as a whole does its work."[5]

Given such an atmosphere as described by Tom Auxter, it is indeed incredible that the philosophy department at the University of Florida works as well as it does. In fact, it is the philosophy department's dissenting colleagues who should be applauded for their efforts to keep alive what remains of the truth-function and discovery methods raised in my earlier remarks about Dewey's mission for the university.

Finally, we should also be reminded of one of Dewey's most memorable and important distinctions: that of ends and means. In his 1902 essay on academic freedom, Dewey notes that "the financial factor in the conduct of the modern university is continually growing in importance, and very serious problems arise in adjusting this factor to strict educational ideals.

Money is absolutely indispensable as a means. ...If the university is to be a true university, money and all things connected therewith must be subordinate. But the pressure to get the means is tending to make it an end; and this academic materialism--is the worst foe of freedom of work in its widest sense."[6]

It is this more invisible hand of freedom that brings me to Adam Smith whose "invisible" pen has perhaps been read far less than Dewey's. As my colleague Kenneth D. McCracken has pointed out,[7] Smith divided occupational life into two basic groups: Productive and non-productive (in modern parlance, "non-productive" might be translated as "service-related" and "perishable"). For Smith, professors clearly belonged in the latter classification. Smith was fitfully disturbed about the apparent lack of motivation provided by occupations, such as college teaching, that had no product. Accordingly, he complained about the pay of professors at the time of his writing of <u>The Wealth of Nations</u> (1776). Success seemed to be in no way related to success or failure in the professor's teaching. Smith also noted that any professor who was moderately hard-working and ambitious would be wise to devote his time and energy to other (more external) activities. At Oxford and other prestigious universities, this circumstance often meant that many professors would not even "go through the pretense of teaching after they had received... tenure."[8] Fighting an uphill battle, Smith expended considerable time and energy in efforts to develop a system in which university professors would be rewarded for their industry.[9]

I exhume Adam Smith merely to remind us of some of the important matters that Professor Auxter seems to be pointing us toward, either implicitly or explicitly: the forgotten hand of the college teacher as a transmittor, conveyor, and explorer of the truth-function of the university--that essential goal to which Dewey reminds us in his essay on academic freedom. We, as professors, leave our mark primarily through the power and service of ideas which, on Adam Smith's terms, may be instantly perishable service items unless they are continually transmitted, explored, and protected by scholar/teachers willing to ply their trade relatively untrammeled by those inevitable local and temporal considerations that make our profession less "unalloyed" and thus less pure. In that respect, Auxter and his colleagues of dissent have been much more loyal and devoted to the university and its ideals than has the president of the University of Florida. The latter may have taken far too seriously the one reference to his institution in Jencks and Riesman's The Academic Revolution (1968) which points to his campus' supposed comparative lack of "excellence" and "national visibility":

> The University of Florida in Gainesville is probably unique in being the only state university in the country that has less academic standing than a newer (formerly all feminine) institution, Florida State in Tallahassee.[10]

I wish Tom Auxter and his colleagues well in their efforts to move beyond such code words as "excellence," "national visibility" and "success" in order to show the University of Florida the way in common canons of academic decency, fair play, diversity and freedom of work for all inhabitants of its institutions as well as our own.

FOOTNOTES

1. John B. Buescher, "The Marriage of Alma Mater to Adam Smith," Thought & Action: The NEA Higher Education Journal, 3, (1987): 48.

2. Thomas Elmer Will, "A Menace to Freedom: The College Trust," reprinted from The Arena, Vol. XXVI (1901), in Walter P. Metzger (Ed.), The American Concept of Academic Freedom in Formation: A Collection of Essays and Reports (New York: Arno Press, 1977), p. 256.

3. John Dewey, "Academic Freedom," reprinted from Educational Review (1902), in Metzger, p. 14.

4. Ibid., p. 3.

5. Ibid., p. 10.

6. Ibid.

7. Kenneth D. McCracken, "Merit Systems: The Resurrection of an Unworkable Past," paper presented at the 1987 meeting of the Southeast Philosophy of Education Society (Jackson, Tennessee, February 6-7, 1987). See also Adam Smith, The Wealth of Nations, pp. 142-143, in Robert Maynard Hutchins (Ed.), Great Books of the Western World, Vol. 39 (Chicago: Encyclopedia Britannica, 1952).

8. Ibid., p. 2.

9. Ibid.

10. Christopher Jencks and David Riesman, The Academic Revolution (New York: Doubleday, 1968), p. 275.

CHAPTER TWO

BERTRAND RUSSELL AND SOME THOUGHTS ON EDUCATION

by

Shirley Jespersen
University of Arkansas, Little Rock

When presented with the theme of this conference, "Thinking About Education: Philosophical Issues and Perspectives," I thought, "What would Bertrand Russell, the subject of my studies for many years, have to say to this august group concerning modern American education?" Moreover, would what he stated over half a century ago have any relevance or applicability today?

But before we address these two questions, let me refresh your memories with a brief biography of Russell.

Background

In 1916, when Bertrand Russell made his first contributions to the field of education theory, he was already widely-known as a mathematician, philosopher, and intellectual par excellence. His long life (1872-1970) can be divided into three major periods, each focused on different concerns. From young adulthood until the completion of Principia Mathematica in 1910, Russell's fundamental preoccupation was intellectual. During his middle years, Russell concerned himself with social issues and wrote extensively on politics, morals, and education. His final decades were spent in widely-publicized opposition to the development of nuclear weapons and to the war in Viet Nam.

Bertrand Arthur William Russell was born on May 18, 1872, to Viscount and Lady Amberley. His father was a member of a distinguished English aristocratic family which included Lord William Russell, executed in 1683 for allegedly plotting to murder King Charles II, and Lord John Russell, twice Prime Minister of Great Britain. Orphaned at the age of four, he and his older brother, Frank, were raised by their grandmother Lady John Russell, at Pembroke Lodge, an eleven acre estate which Queen Victoria had given to Lord John Russell for his services to the crown. At the age of eleven, young Bertrand began studying Euclidean geometry under his brother's tutelage. Russell later recalled this as one of the great events of his life, "...as dazzling as first love."[1] Young Bertrand was educated at home until he entered Cambridge in 1890 to study mathematics and philosophy. For a decade after graduating, he continued to study and write in both fields. This period of his life culminated in the publication of Principia Mathematica (1910-1913), a three-volume work co-authored with Alfred North Whitehead, which greatly influenced Western philosophy.

During his middle years, Russell turned from primarily intellectual and academic concerns to social, political, and educational issues. He became a strong advocate of social reform and wrote numerous articles and books, expressing his deep concern for the human condition and advancing reforms which were considered provocative and radical by many of his readers. After his two youngest children were born, in the early 1920's, Russell's interest in education predominated, and he wrote two major works and numerous articles on the subject. In 1927, Russell and his second wife, Dora, put his ideas into practice at their Beacon Hill School.

In 1931, Russell's second marriage ended, and with it, any further involvement with Beacon Hill. He spent the summer of 1932 at his home in Cornwall writing Education and the Social Order, his final major contribution to the field of education. He then turned his interest to other areas, while Dora Russell continued to run the school, first alone, and then with her second husband. In 1943, the War Office took over the school, fearing a German invasion of Penzance, the area where the school had been relocated.

Russell's Thoughts on Education

Russell's thoughts on education can best be examined within the context of the activities at his Beacon Hill School. The school was founded because Russell and his wife were critical of both the traditional and progressive schools in existence at the time. They considered traditional British schools unsuitable because, as Russell put it, "...old-fashioned education at bottom only recognized one thing as essential--that a child should learn by beating and dogmatic instruction from his elders what was his duty to his parents and society, and in most cases to his God."[2] The progressive schools of the time were also unsuitable because they did not sufficiently stress the importance of acquiring knowledge. Thus, on one hand, the Russells disliked religious instruction, prudery, and the many restraints on freedom that were taken for granted in conventional schools. On the other hand, they could not agree with most progressive educators who advocated complete absence of discipline,[3] and who thought academic instruction was unimportant. What the Russells desired was an unusual combination at that time: a school that emphasized the teaching of a traditional curriculum in a progressive environment.

Russell was convinced that a careful, systematic approach to learning a discipline was necessary. He stated that mere freedom to play about with the materials of the arts and sciences was not sufficient. Much exact knowledge was required to cope with modern civilization and it could "...only be acquired by application."[4] This belief that knowledge was possible, but difficult, gave his theory of education a decidedly traditional orientation.

It is interesting to speculate, at this point, how Russell would react to recent events in American education, more specifically, the whole issue of what should be stressed in our college curricula. I strongly suspect that Russell would support Professor Allan Bloom[5] and those who believe that college youth should be required to learn the great ideas of the western world in their historical context. I believe he would endorse the position of Isaac D. Barchas,[6] an undergraduate in classics at Stanford University, who recently deplored the impending replacement of the one-year required Western Culture course, the university's version of the Great Books program, with a course which would stress diverse ideas and values, and emphasize the last six to eight centuries. At the same time, Russell would caution that education was not to aim at preserving the past, but towards the world that was envisioned for the future. He stated that education "...should be inspired, not by a regretful hankering after the extinct beauties of Greece and the Renaissance, but a shining vision of the society that is to be...."[7]

Russell, it must be remembered, was a social reconstructionist who saw education as the key to reforming existing institutions, thereby creating a better society.

More significant than his position on the curriculum, however, were Russell's ideas on the type of environment that would be most conducive to learning. Beacon Hill School was based on the concept that the rights of the individual were to be respected in the educational process. This concept of respect for the child was the justification for some educational practices that were considered radical at that time. For example, the school was run by a School Council which comprised the entire school staff, from the headmaster (Russell) to the janitor, and all children five years old and older. Each member of the Council participated in making rules concerning bedtimes, personal hygiene, cleaning up, unkindness, bullying, destructiveness, and so on. The adults were charged with enforcing the rules to avoid the practice, common in British schools at that time, of putting older children in authority, which frequently led to bullying and coercion.[8]

Because Russell was highly critical of the vast system of competitiveness existing in the educational institutions of his day, competition was not encouraged at Beacon Hill. Russell believed that competition was not only bad as an educational fact, but also as an ideal for the young to emulate. What the world needed, said Russell, was not competition but organization and cooperation.[9]

Consequently, no prizes were given at Beacon Hill, and end of term examinations were only occasionally administered. What competition there was, was limited to an occasional test, class game, or exhibits of the children's work. In spite of the attempts to minimize competition, the school was not entirely immune from the constraints imposed by British social and educational traditions. Dora Russell complained that were it not for the pressure of examinations and class differences, the children would have been allowed to specialize more than they were able to and to follow whatever bent they had. Had society permitted, Beacon Hill would have been as content to turn out good mechanics or carpenters as mathematicians.[10]

At Beacon Hill students had complete freedom of thought and expression.[11] Their choice of words or topics were neither censored nor restricted. They were allowed to be irreverent toward adults, including their teachers. Swearing was not forbidden, neither were discussions of sex or other controversial subjects.

Similarly, children were allowed to express their opinions on religion, politics, morals, or any other topic, whether their opinions were popular or not.

Russell's advocacy of free speech was based on his own experiences and on his support of the empirical theory of knowledge. Reflections on his youth, when open discussions on many topics were forbidden at Pembroke Lodge because they offended his grandmother, persuaded Russell not to restrict his students' or his own children's speech. His happy memories of the years at Cambridge, where he freely discussed all types of topics without any fear of censorship, also influenced him. Additionally, and most importantly, Russell's advocacy of empiricism led him to conclude that everyone, even a child, was entitled to freedom of thought and expression. Moreover, Russell viewed knowledge not as a prescribed body of systematically organized facts and concepts to be mastered by the student, but as tentatively held opinions "...with a consciousness that new evidence may at any moment lead to their abandonment."[12] He believed that the purpose of education was to encourage children to think for themselves rather than to compel them to hold positive opinions on doubtful matters. Education was to foster a desire for truth, not the conviction that some particular creed was the truth. These goals could not be achieved if the students' speech or thought was censored.

This, of course, brings to mind another current controversy in American education, namely, whether students are, indeed, entitled to the same First Amendment rights as adults. Just recently, in the case Hazelwood School District v. Kuhlmeier, the Supreme Court, in a 5 to 3 ruling, upheld a school principal's right to censor a student newspaper. The case involved a publication called Spectrum, produced by journalism students at Hazelwood East High School near St. Louis. In 1983, the principal ordered two articles deleted from the paper. One had to do with three students who had become pregnant; the other dealt with the impact of divorce on students. Three students who worked on the Spectrum brought suit, alleging a violation of their First Amendment right to free expression. Justice Byron White, writing for the majority, ruled that educators may exert editorial control "...so long as their actions are reasonably related to legitimate pedagogical concerns."[13] Justice William Brennan, in a stinging dissent, charged that the principal had

"...violated the First Amendment's prohibitions against censorship of any student expression that neither disrupts classwork nor invades the rights of others." He went on to say that the decision could convert public schools into "...enclaves of totalitarianism...that strangle the free mind at its source."[14]

Russell would most certainly have supported the students' right to free expression. He believed that intelligence and honestly would be warped if students always had to consider how a question they wanted to ask would be received, or whether they dare speak a thought which was on their minds. Suppressing speech was galling to the young and likely to produce sullen and stupid docility. Moreover, intellectual honesty was a more valuable quality to Russell than insincere manners.[15]

Conclusion

The Beacon Hill experiment took place over 50 years ago, yet it anticipated two recent major recommendations to improve American education in the last years of the 20th century. First, the school emphasized academic rigor and competence. An accomplished scholar himself, Russell knew that if advances were to be made in any given discipline, individuals had to undergo a prolonged period of thorough, systematic, and disciplined training. He also believed that education should promote the love of mental adventure. To this end, the students at Beacon Hill were encouraged to exhibit qualities which Russell believed were desirable and essential to the successful pursuit of knowledge: curiosity, open-mindedness, patience, industry, concentration, exactness, and the belief that knowledge was possible, though difficult.[16]

The importance of emphasizing academic competence has been acknowledged by a number of well-publicized, nation-wide studies of the American public school system, most notably the National Commission on Excellence in Education.[17] It appears that our schools have fallen short in maintaining and promoting high levels of academic performance and American society is paying a heavy price. Excellence is now, as the publicity has it, at the forefront of every educator's agenda. Russell might add that it always should have been.

Second, Russell suggested that academic training take place under more humane and psychologically sound conditions than were found in the schools of his era. Beacon Hill had the type of learning environment believed by present-day humanists[18] to be most conducive to preparing youngsters for effective participation in society. It emphasized developing self-discipline and responsibility for one's actions in a democratically organized environment. It encouraged students to think and work for themselves without the pressures found in conventional British schools. The teacher was at the periphery of the learning process, allowing the children to be actively engaged in their own education. Most of all, the child was respected as a worthwhile member of the educational enterprise known as Beacon Hill.

A little more than half a century has passed since Bertrand Russell formulated his views on the nature and goals of education. At the time, he was living in an Old World society that was just beginning to come to terms with the realities of the modern, industrial age. The old regimes with their aristocracies, their hereditary monarchies, and their prescriptive rights were slowly being replaced by more democratic institutions. Those who had enjoyed a monopoly of power and privilege were being challenged by new classes demanding their rightful share of the goods, rights, and benefits of society. The traditional goals and practices of institutions, including educational institutions, were being questioned. In this unsettled social and intellectual milieu, Russell proposed a theoretical framework for a modern educational system that would not only meet the needs of the individual, but also the needs of an increasingly complex and dangerous world.

Has the passage of over five decades diminished the importance of Russell's contributions to education? This short study suggests that there are a number of components that are as valid, relevant, and applicable today as they were in Russell's time. In conclusion, there still exists a rich Russellian legacy for American educators to consider and, perhaps, to finally put into practice.

FOOTNOTES

1. Bertrand Russell, The Autobiography of Bertrand Russell (London: Unwin, 1975), p. 30.

2. Bertrand Russell, "In our School," New Republic, 68 (September 9, 1931), p. 92.

3. Russell, The Autobiography, p. 387.

4. Russell, "In our School," p. 93.

5. Allan Bloom, The Closing of the American Mind (New York: Simon & Schuster, 1987).

6. Isaac D. Barchas, "Stanford Would Toss Intellectual Heritage to the Winds," Wall Street Journal (January 21, 1988), p. 30.

7. Bertrand Russell, "Education as a Political Institution," Atlantic Monthly, 117. (June, 1916), p. 757.

8. Dora Russell, "Beacon Hill," in The Modern Schools Handbook, ed. Trevor Blewitt (London: Victor Gollancz, 1934), pp. 36-37.

9. Bertrand Russell, Education and the Social Order (London: Alen & Unwin, 1932), p. 177.

10. Dora Russell, "Beacon Hill," pp. 35-36.

11. Bertrand Russell, "Free Speech in Childhood," The New Statesman and Nation, 1 (May 30, 1931), p. 485.

12. Bertrand Russell, Unpopular Essays (New York: Simon & Schuster, 1951), p. 15.

13. "Stop the Student Presses," Time (January 25, 1988), p. 54.

14. "A Limit on the Student Press," Newsweek (January 25, 1988), p. 60.

15. Russell, "In our School," p. 93.

16. Bertrand Russell, Education and the Good Life (New York: Boni & Liveright, 1926), p. 243.

17. National Commission on Excellence in Education, *A Nation at Risk: The Imperative for Educational Reform* (Washington, D.C.: U.S. Government Printing Office, 1983), p. 5.

18. Arthur W. Combs, "What the Future Demands of Education," *Phi Delta Kappan*, 62 (January 1981).

CHAPTER TWO

LEARNING TO BE TOGETHER: JOHN DEWEY'S THEORY OF EXPERIENCE, GROUP DYNAMICS AND EXPERIENTIAL EDUCATION AS CONCEPTUAL FOUNDATIONS

by

Judy Vogt
The University of West Florida

In today's world of interdependence, much of our lives is spent in groups--at home, work, school, and play. People learning, working, creating, and living together is a foundation for modern existence. Knowing more about groups in numerous contexts and how we exist within them is an important educational objective for now and the future. Thus, educators are actively examining how to educate people to "be together." Two factors clearly emerge as we consider this educational responsibility--group dynamics and experiential learning. Both of these elements were integrated in the 1960s in a teaching-learning format called the Training Group.* It is my view that the T-group continues to be the most useful and pedagogical sound means for teaching people to be together. This paper assumes the T-group's worth and at the same time strengthens that assumption by examining John Dewey's theory of experience as added philosophical and theoretical justification.

To proceed then, the paper will first present overview discussions of Dewey's theory of experience and T-group methodology; it will continue by enumerating and clarifying several dimensions of Dewey's theory and examining in a one-to-one manner how the T-group meets these criteria and thus demonstrating how John Dewey's theory of experience serves as a philosophical and theoretical justification for teaching people about group dynamics in this experiential way.

---

* Hereafter the Training Group will be called T-group. Other currently used names for similar learning formats are group development, team building, and growth groups.

Dewey's Theory of Experience

The crux of this paper will come after these two initial steps; this section and the one to follow are attempts to provide a frame of reference for understanding the final analysis. In the last part of this essay the more complex aspects and issues of the theory of experience and the T-group method will be considered.

Because the emphasis of the paper is on the educational value of T-groups, Dewey's philosophy of experience must be examined in the context of education. This is not a difficult task because Dewey's chief philosophical interest was in education. "The underlying unity of Dewey's philosophy of education is that there is a close and necessary relation between the processes of actual experience and education."[1] His suggestion was that education be based on personal experience.

It is obvious, however, that all experiences are not educative in the ways deemed useful, valuable, and "right," for living in society. Dewey stated that the central problem of an education based on experience is to select the kinds of experiences that live fruitfully and creatively in subsequent experiences. Here there are two points to be made. One is that of selecting experiences and suggests something about the role of the teacher--the role of the teacher is to select the "proper" experiences and to guide learners toward the "proper" outcomes. The second point to be made concerns the first of Dewey's criteria for a valuable educational experience--the criterion of continuity. Dewey asserts that every experience "takes up something from those which have gone on before and modifies in some way the quality of those which will come after."[2] If this is continuity, what does it suggest about the quality of an experience? The "proper" or good experience according to Dewey is one that reinforces the individual's initiative and gives the person enough power and desire to go forward. Vague as the last part of this statement is, it helps us to see the importance Dewey placed on each present experience in forming and affecting future experiences.

The second criterion of experience is interaction. By this Dewey means there are two elements necessary in order to have an experience--internal and objective conditions. Interaction is always going on within the individual (internal conditions) and between or among things and/or other persons (objective conditions). Thus, there are two sources of experience--from within the person and from the environment. The key concern of the educator, keeping in mind the criterion of interaction, is to determine what factors in the environment can be best utilized in an experience for the growth of the individual.

The last point for consideration in this brief sketch of Dewey's theory of experience is his view that in education there is an "...intimate and indissoluble connection of means used and ends reached."[3] In other words, each experience is both the means and goal of education. Education (by experience) is an ongoing process whereby knowledge is accumulated as an instrument for intelligent living and further inquiry. Experiences have educative value to the extent that they are based on the continuity of knowledge--i.e., knowledge which modifies attitudes and skills. Worthwhile experiences, in order to ensure continuity of knowledge, must involve the individual and the individual's whole physical and social environment. Summing up this view of education as both the ends and means via experience, Dewey states specifically that an experience is valuable when it promotes self-control, judgement, ability to evaluate and use ideas, contributes to problem-solving, and leads to further experience. And, finally Dewey states that "Education should adopt a systematic experimental approach to the development of experience."[4]

The T-group Method

Before beginning this description of the T-group, it is necessary to point out that "...There has never been any complete statement of the method."[5] It becomes a difficult task to say "This is what a T-group is." The following is an effort to provide the reader with some of the basic aspects of this technique as this author perceives them. "Each trainer has his [her] own concept of the method...."[6]

The T-group method is the most important design or learning experience used by those interested in group dynamics to teach their findings. It is an experiential method. This technique has three major purposes: 1) to give its members training in the understanding and skills of human relations; 2) to provide its members with effective ways of working together by associations, agencies, and groups in communities, states, regions, and countries; 3) to improve group efficiency in decision-making and production. The T-group is considered to be the most effective way of bringing about learning in these areas according to its adherents.

To achieve the aforementioned aims, individuals must be trained in analysis, planning, evaluation, and action skills. Research has shown that merely telling people (whether combined with discussion or not) does not provide individuals with these kinds of abilities. Analysis and other skills necessary must be <u>practiced</u> and feedback must be given as to the progress an individual is making so that the person can improve on or change his/her behavior. (It is assumed, at this point, that members involved in this training want to achieve these aims.) Therefore, mere case analysis is not enough. One, it does not allow learners to try new behaviors and two, it is dealing with static situations. This latter point needs a word of clarification. If one's aim is to improve human relations, static-situation analysis falls short of it. This is because group relations are dynamic and ongoing.

The way, then, to provide for the <u>learning</u> of these skills is to use the learning group itself as the laboratory of study. "The T-group provides participants with the experiences of constructing without blueprint or direction an organism which has goals, structure, procedures, standards, and other elements of group life."[7] "In the area of human relations, (on-going) individual and group processes become the curriculum."[8] The T-group provides trainees with an opportunity to try new behavior, to secure feedback on their behavior, to experiment with new ideas of leadership and membership, and to develop an awareness of the problems of group organization, functioning, and growth--on a personal level as well as on an intellectual level. This latter distinction refers to the comment concerning the research which finds the lecture or lecture-discussion method to be inappropriate for certain kinds of learnings. These learnings, specifically, are changes in behavior. Basic educational psychology shows that in order for changes in behavior to occur, an individual must be emotionally involved in a situation and this is what is meant by involving the trainee on a feeling level.

The last point for consideration is the role of the trainer (facilitator or group leader) in the T-group. Basically, his/her task is to see to it that the group has significant experiences in trying to work together and that conditions are such that people can learn from these experiences. The trainer definitely has a certain amount of control of the group in that activities planned to satisfy needs of the group are trainer-approved. "The trainers do not tell the group what to do, but help them to analyze their behavior."[9] These last two comments are not contradictory because it is the methods of analysis which are trainer-approved and they are approved only if they are conducive to the learning of the members.

The following comments summarize the T-group method of teaching. T-groups (these are small groups, the ideal size being six to eighteen members) use the members as laboratory subjects for the study of forces affecting group behavior. At the same time, each group has set up small experiments within itself to test new ways of working together or of producing change in a group situation. The trainer's function is to provide help and some guidelines for carrying out the process. "The primary target of change is the trainee's competence as a participant in groups; the secondary target is the groups to which the trainees will return after training."[10]

The T-group As a Valuable Learning Activity According to Dewey's Criteria

Some introductory statements to this section are necessary and helpful. The first is that to this author's knowledge, there has been no previous attempt to philosophically justify the T-group method according to John Dewey's theory of experience. But the doors are opened for this kind of analysis by Dewey himself. "It sounds academic to say that substantial battering of social relations waits upon the growth of a scientific social psychology."[11] This appears to be one of his major goals. The underlying assumption of this paper is that John Dewey is responsible for the development of a scientific social psychology and, to be more specific, the development of the T-group method can be directly attributed to his philosophically-psychologically based ideas. The remainder of this paper will be devoted to the verification of the preceding point. The means by which this will be accomplished is as follows. First, Dewey's views concerning a major issue in his theory of experience will be considered. Second, after Dewey's criteria are examined, aspects of the T-group method which will fulfill his criteria will be presented. Concepts to be analyzed are 1) the means-and-ends concept; 2) process including feedback, interaction, conflict, and content; 3) reality in experience; 4) relevance; 5) social relations; 6) change; 7) democracy and freedom; 8) the role of the teacher; and 9) learning, defined as the process plus the outcome.

It should be pointed out that neither Dewey's theory nor in discussion of T-groups are these concepts dealt with separately from one another. This is an attempt to extrapolate these issues and what has been said about them to deal with concrete terms and to organize the discussion in a meaningful way. The method of extrapolation was to choose key issues of both Dewey's theory and the T-group method and then to compare each. It is quite relevant to the aim of this paper to state that without exception there was a one to one relationship of the major concepts involved in each of these; what was a key concept in Dewey's work was a key concept in the T-group method and vice versa. Thus, even before examining the specific concepts in this analysis, there is an obvious awareness that the two are intricately related.

The first consideration will be the means-and-ends concept because it is the framework around which all else is built in Dewey's theory of experience and the T-group method. By looking at experience as the means and ends of education Dewey is asserting that knowledge gained from an experience is transformed into instruments which are used for two things: 1) intelligent living and 2) further inquiry. Each experience provides the learners with information they can use thereafter (ends) and with information which will lead them to other experiences for more learning (means).

> Now, old experience is used to suggest aims and methods for developing a new and improved experience....We do not merely have to respect the past, or wait for accidents to force change upon us. We use our past experiences to construct new and better ones in the future. The very fact of

47

experience thus includes the process by which it directs itself in its own betterment.[12]

Speaking more directly on means, Dewey says that the "...result of an experience is a vast complex of objects, qualities, events, meanings, and habits which determine some future response....And when experience is controlled by the method of sciences, it yields that knowledge of the workings of things which furnishes us with the power to shape the course of events."[13] It seems that Dewey's basic assumption is that there is a continuity between knowing (gained from experiences) and evaluating future experiences.

It seems quite clear that the T-group fulfills this means-and ends criterion. A T-group has "... the practical goal of improving future behavior (means) as well as the intellectual task of understanding why people do what they do...."[14] This method is an attempt to provide for research and training in the problems of bringing about group growth. The way members achieve the above goals is by investigating the processes of communication, influence, and social problems. They do this by "...sharing in the diagnosis of the problems and decision as to the direction and kind of change, needed, as well as in carrying out the change."[15] The most important element in change (or learning) is emotional involvement, for only then can there be an experience which fulfills the means-and-ends criterion. As Dewey says, "Emotions are not private--they are occurrences in the development of experience to some issue of conclusion....Experience means primarily not knowledge, but the ways of doing and suffering."[16]

Human beings, according to Dewey, are creatures who although bound by the antecedent conditions of their existence can within limits redirect and redetermine both the world and themselves and become morally responsible for those things which their thought and action can influence. There is no doubt that the scientists in group dynamics feel the same way and they have developed a process whereby individuals are taken from their present state and provided with the tools and feelings they need to improve human relations. The process is an experience which gives them both the knowledge (ends) and skills (means) developed through scientific and emotional involvement, to carry out their aims.

The second point for consideration deals with aspects of the <u>process</u> of experience--feedback, interaction, conflict and content. According to Dewey:

> Experience involves change, but change is a meaningless transition unless it is consciously connected with the return of consequences which flow from it. When an activity is continued into the undergoing of consequences, when the change made by action is reflected back into a change made in us, we learn something.[17]

Trying something is only <u>doing</u> something; undergoing the consequences of what was tried in instruction is a second phase. Clearly, it is this "undergoing of consequences" which T-group members call feedback. "Every group is able to improve its ability to operate as a group to the extent that it consciously examines its processes and their consequences with improved processes."[18] A person with a commitment to change will <u>learn</u> not just from trying new behaviors. He/she must <u>also</u> get "feedback" from others about how these new behaviors affected them and the self.

If this is so, then a necessary part of learning is interaction with others and/or environment. "Experience is a dynamic affair which is reciprocal and constituted by all the modes of intercourse between a conscious being and the environment, both physical and social."[19] In the learning process, "the experiencing organism is not a passive receiver but a dynamic participant in a moving, developing situation."[20] To Dewey, the name given to all that passes between the organism and its surroundings is interaction.

The T-group method is based to a large extent on interaction. The purpose of social interaction is to increase learning. Limits are thus set on the kind of interaction which is worthwhile. "The quality of interaction is good when it is appropriate to the task and to the purposes."[21] It becomes useful to reflect on one of the aims of the T-group method--to improve human relations. One aspect of better human relations is better social interaction. Interaction, it must be realized, can hinder or aid one's relations with others. Only by practice and feedback can one learn this and can one learn <u>what kinds</u> of interaction are

49

purposeful. According to Dewey, experience stands for all commerce between the person and his/her environment; but to be significant and educational, the individual must react to it with an informed <u>awareness</u> of the problems and challenge of his environment. The T-group method affords the individual the chance to take part in the process of interaction while at the same time it helps the person to realize the importance of interaction in human relations. It is truly an educative experience.

An aspect of interaction is conflict. The T-group's action is centered around the resolution of conflict. Conflict is often a catalyst for learning. The experiential method is sometimes referred to as the method of dealing with conflicts. Dewey provided, too, for this orientation towards conflict when he stated that real learning results from a "blocking of habitual conduct." Through interaction, invariably a problem or conflict occurs. It is by working with and solving this problem that learning takes place. Intricately related to this is the importance of emotional involvement as mentioned earlier. The reason why conflict leads to learning is that it gets the learner emotionally involved. The only "...genuine learning situation is one which involves the emotions of the learner...."[22]

What then should be the content of an experience? Dewey says that there should be "...no distinction of subject matter and method....Experience itself is educative."[23] The experience is the subject matter. The subject matter is not knowledge, he says, but "ways of doing." The subject matter of the T-group is its own processes. The experience itself is what is focused upon and is the subject matter. "...The most useful content of experience...is the feelings the individual is aware of."[24]

The concept of reality brings together the aspects of feedback, interaction, conflict and content. To Dewey, the kinds of experiences which are most valuable to the individual are those which are real--these are affairs which are complex and which consist of many variables. If such experiences are isolated from the reality of participating in them then the special characteristics of the subject matter are destroyed. Thus, in order for learning to occur, an experience must be reality-centered. "The experiential approach is a way to get the data needed to interpret reality, and it makes the collection of such data a part of the action itself."[25] It is possible to generalize from what is learned in the T-group because it is real. It does not deal with the aspects of living in isolation -it is an experience of living. It consists of interaction between the individual and his/her environment and living with the consequences of the interaction. In the T-group it is this interaction-and-its-consequences process which is the content for learning. The T-group fulfills Dewey's criterion of reality in experience.

> If we frame our conception of knowledge on the experimental model, we find that it is a way of operating upon and with the things of ordinary experience so that we can frame our ideas of them in terms of their interaction with one another, instead of in terms of the qualities they directly present, and that thereby our control of them, our ability to change them and direct their changes as we desire, is indefinitely increased. It is the way of interaction by which other natural interactions become subject to direction.[26]

The aims of Dewey's theory of experience and the T-group method are inseparable from and interwoven with the issue of social relations and democracy. Training has two basic aims--to improve skills in human relations and to improve group leadership. The aim of experience is to improve an individual's ability to live constructively and/or efficiently in society. In the aims of both of these, the concept of change is central.

According to Dewey, "custom is essentially a fact of associated living whose force is dominant in forming the habits of individuals."[27]

> The formation of habits of belief, desire and judgement is going on at every instant under the influence of the conditions set by human contact, intercourse, and associations with one another.[28]

If improvement of social relations in order to live more efficiently in society is our goal, it becomes necessary to deal with individuals in group settings. This is precisely the theoretical assumption of group dynamics and T-group advocates.

> The behavior, attitudes, beliefs, and values of an individual are firmly grounded in the groups to which he [she] belongs. They are properties of groups and of the relationships amongst people. Whether people change or resist change, therefore, will be greatly influenced by the nature of these groups. Attempts to change these behaviors, etc., must be concerned with the dynamics of groups.[29]

Dewey goes on to say that "...there is no group at any time or place which does not have some code of manners...it is a uniform attendant of all social relationships."[30] Group dynamics calls this code of manners norms. In the process of changing people's behavior through the groups to which they belong, one of the key areas of focus is the rules of conduct they have set up for themselves. These norms control behavior, but they are usually intrinsic to a situation and members often are not really aware of them. Oftentimes, too, certain norms are prompted from past experiences and often they are developed in a group which are not appropriate to it. Dewey suggests there is a "...need for the development of forms of intercourse that are inherently appropriate to the social situations"[31] unique in each group. To change group behavior, group norms must be the first target- to be the first target, people must be made aware of them.

In a democracy, the concept of change takes on new dimensions "...the essence of democratic change lies in the need for all concerned to share in the diagnosis of the problems and decisions as to the direction and kind of change as well as in carrying out the change."[32] To Dewey,

> ...democratic social arrangements promote a better quality of experience, one which is more widely accessible and enjoyable,

> than non-democratic forms of social
> life....The principle of regard for
> individual freedom and for decency
> and kindliness of human relations
> comes back in the end to the
> conviction that these are tributary
> to a higher quality of experience
> on the part of a greater number
> than are the methods of repression
> and coercion or force. The reason
> for our preference is that we
> believe that mutual consultation
> and convictions reached through
> discussion and analysis make
> possible a better quality of
> experience than can otherwise be
> provided on any wide scale....An
> experience must rely upon and use
> the humane methods which are based
> on democracy....[33]

Hence, the foundations of democracy become very dependent on groups for their existence and implementation. In fact, it is within the context of groups that consideration must be given to a major tenet of democracy--freedom.

As has already been discussed, the individual is decidedly a product of his/her environment and/or social interactions. How, then, can humans be free?

> Regarding freedom, the important
> thing to bear in mind is that it
> designates a mental attitude rather
> than external unconstraint of
> movements, but that this quality of
> mind cannot develop without a fair
> leeway of movements in exploration,
> experimentation, application, etc.[34]

An experience must provide the individual with opportunities to be free; it must also provide the person with the tools and habits to think freely. The T-group situation rests heavily upon the realization that human beings need support in order to feel free to experiment with new behaviors and each group spends a great deal of time building supportive relationships. This does not mean that everyone will agree with an individual's actions or point of view, but it does mean that they will develop an awareness that he/she has the right (freedom) to try to express them within limits. (Refer to the section on "proper" behaviors for discussion of what is meant by "within limits" here.) In the end, T-group members come to the realization that in order for better group and human relations to come about, each person must feel free to express him/herself. The development of a supportive atmosphere in a group leads to freedom which leads to improved social relations. The T-group thus promotes "...the development of practical skills of free and democratic action and thought."[35]

Another aspect of democracy and/or freedom is leadership. Group dynamics views leadership in functional terms. In other words, group dynamics as a body of knowledge or a field of study views leadership in many ways, but the most prevalent way is by functional role. The leader is not determined by status or personality; he/she is determined by the task being performed--i.e., who is best able to provide the particular function needed by the group in achieving this task.

> In order to train leaders in a democracy we must find methods of encouraging ways of leadership which move groups to decide and act effectively and which help groups to grow in the process of action. Thus leadership training in a democracy is group education, which gives wisdom to confer leadership, and wisdom to accept and act for the group.[36]

Democratic action also involves cooperation and the citizenship role. The essence of the cooperative relationship is two-way communication; it is possible only when individuals have purposes in common and recognize the need they have for each other. When cooperative and collaborative attitudes exist, a group becomes active and pours its efforts into problem-solving activities. In both training and educational activities, people "...learn from experience that interdependence exists and that they are a part of it. And thus they have consciousness of their citizenship role."[37]

Democratic action and thought are bound up in group relationships. In order to bring about democracy, freedom, leadership, cooperation, and citizenship, each must be provided for in democratic terms. The only way this can occur, according to the theory of experience and the T-group method, is by the analysis of what goes on in groups; this is called "processing" the group or the activity or an event. When there is effective group behavior--and if freedom, functional leadership and cooperation exist--democracy at its best will be in operation.

The role of the teacher-trainer in this experiencing process is now to be considered. According to Dewey, the classroom should become a group or community held together by participation in common activities in order to fulfill the criterion of realism. This being the case, the primary source of control is to be found in the very nature of the tasks in which it is involved. The role of the teacher in such instance is to have a knowledge of 1) individuals and 2) the subject matter so that activities can be selected "...which lend themselves to social organization, an organization in which all individuals have an opportunity to contribute something, and in which the activities in which all participate are the chief carriers of control."[38] Further, the teacher has a responsibility for the conduct of the interactions which are the very life of the group; the teacher should take on the role of leader of group activities. Also, the teacher must provide the conditions which stimulate thinking and he/she must take on a sympathetic attitude toward the activities of the learners by entering into common experience with them. "In such shared activity, the teacher is a learner and the learner is a teacher...."[39] Finally, the teacher has the responsibility for instituting the conditions for the kind of present experience which has a favorable effect upon the future. To summarize, the teacher's role is to see to it that "education as growth or maturity is an ever-present process."[40]

The major role of the trainer is to help the group grow. He/she does this by helping the group develop the power to use the experiential method. He/she guides the group toward self-direction, efficiency, the ability to cope with frustration, skill in avoiding realistically anticipated failure, the ability to channel spontaneously expressed emotion into work, flexibility in designing plans to fit changed situations, rapidity in recovering from emotionally destructive periods, meeting individual needs within the context of group problem solving activities, and finally toward being able to define group problems realistically and in dynamic terms--that is, in terms of what is "really" going on. The reason for this lengthy statement is to show the reader how extensively the trainer's role is similar to the teacher's role as conceptualized in Dewey's theory of experience. This point is further substantiated by the following statement. The trainer's role is three-fold:

> ...first, to help the group have significant experiences together; second, to help the group understand what is happening during these experiences; and third, to help the group relate these ideas about its own experiences to a general methodology for group problem solving.[41]

Summary and Conclusion

In reviewing Dewey's theory of experience and T-group constructs, a clear definition and the value of experiential education emerges. It is also clear that experiential education is especially relevant to the teaching of group dynamics and to helping people learn
...about self
...about self in relation to others
...about groups
...and about one's connection with society at large.

The aim of this discussion has been to show that the experiential T-group method used for teaching people how to be more effective leaders and members of a group can be philosophically--and psychologically -justified as a valuable learning activity according to John Dewey's theory of experience. It is shown that an experience must be reality-centered and must involve the individual emotionally as well as cognitively. The basis for learning is the experience itself. Each experience must build on what the individual is at a given point in time. It must provide the person with knowledge which he/she can use thereafter and a desire to seek new information. It must provide the individual with knowledge and tools, specifically, which will enable him/her to deal wisely and humanely with social situations. An experience must include problem-solving activities and democratic tenets. Each experience should have as its aim the promotion of the growth of its participants. The role of the guide is to provide the conditions necessary for this growth to take place. This is what John Dewey believes will make for a good and/or valuable learning experience. It is precisely these criteria on which the T-group is founded. "It is experience that is directive, it is experience that teaches...."[42]

John Dewey and many experts in the T-group method have based their lives' work on the notion that only through realistic experiences will valuable learning take place. Their efforts have been devoted to this belief with the hope that the individual:

> ...through various avenues of interpretation of experience will gradually begin to nail down a basic methodology of human interaction and, with this, the possibilities of a better world for all of us.[43]

FOOTNOTES

1. Stanley N. Worton, Review Notes and Study Guide to the Major Works of John Dewey (New York: Monarch Press, 1964), p. 92.

2. Ibid., p. 93.

3. John Dewey on Education--Selected Writings (New York: Random House, Inc., 1964), p. 167.

4. John Dewey, Experience and Education (New York: Macmillan Co., 1938), p. 89.

5. Herbert A. Thelen, Dynamics of Groups at Work (Chicago: The University of Chicago Press, 1954), p. 129.

6. Ibid., p. 129.

7. Ibid., p. 67.

8. Faculty of the Training Laboratory in Group Development, Group Growth and Educational Dynamics (Washington, D.C.: NEA and Research Center for Group Dynamics, 1984), p. 6.

9. Malcolm Knowles and Hulda Knowles, *Introduction to Group Dynamics* (New York: Association Press, 1959), p. 67.

10. Herbert A. Thelen, *Dynamics of Groups at Work* (Chicago: The University of Chicago Press, 1954), p. 128.

11. John Dewey, *Human Nature and Conduct* (New York: Henry Holt & Company, 1922), p. 323.

12. John Blewett (Ed.) *John Dewey: His Thought and Influence* (New York: Fordham University Press, 1960), p. 208.

13. Charles W. Hendel (Ed.) *John Dewey and the Experimental Spirit in Philosophy* (New York: The Liberal Arts Press, Inc., 1959), p. 109.

14. Dorothy H. Curtis (Ed.) *Forces in Community Development* (Washington, D.C.: N.T.L.-N.E.A., 1961), p. 48.

15. Leland P. Bradford, *Group Dynamics and Education* (Washington, D.C.: National Education Association, 1948), p. 72.

16. Ibid., p. 112.

17. Ralph B. Winn (Ed.) *John Dewey: Dictionary of Education* (New York: Philosophical Library, 1959), p. 87.

18. Malcolm Knowles and Hulda Knowles *Introduction to Group Dynamics* (New York: Association Press, 1959), p. 67.

19. Charles W. Hendel (Ed.) *John Dewey and the Experimental Spirit in Philosophy* (New York: The Liberal Arts Press, Inc., 1959), p. 181.

20. George C. Geiger, *John Dewey in Perspective* (New York: Oxford University Press, 1958), p. 39.

21. Herbert A. Thelen, *Dynamics of Groups at Work* (Chicago: The University of Chicago Press, 1954), p. 98.

22. Ibid., p. 47.

23. John Blewett (Ed.) *John Dewey: His Thought and Influence* (New York: Fordham University Press, 1960), p. 72.

24. Herbert A. Thelen, *Dynamics of Groups at Work* (Chicago: The University of Chicago Press, 1954), p. 49.

25. Ibid., p. 299.

26. John Dewey, *The Quest for Certainty*, Op. Cit., p. 110.

27. John Dewey, *Human Nature and Conduct* (New York: Henry Holt & Company, 1922), p. 102.

28. Ibid., p. 105.

29. Dorothy H. Curtis (Ed.) *Forces in Community Development* (Washington, D.C.: N.T.L.-N.E.A., 1961), p. 18.

30. John Dewey, *Experience and Education* (New York: Macmillan Co., 1938), p. 59.

31. Ibid., p. 59.

32. Leland P. Bradford, *Group Dynamics and Education* (Washington, D.C.: National Education Association, 1948), p. 79.

33. John Dewey, *Experience and Education* (New York: Macmillan Company, 1938), pp. 34-35.

34. John Dewey, *Democracy and Education* (New York: Macmillan Company, 1916), p. 305.

35. Leland P. Bradford, *Group Dynamics and Education* (Washington, D.C.: National Education Association, 1948), p. 207.

36. Ibid., pp. 180-181.

37. Ibid., p. 29.

38. John Dewey, *Experience and Education* (New York: Macmillan Company, 1938), p. 56.

39. John Dewey, *Democracy and Education* (New York: Macmillan, 1916), p. 160.

40. John Dewey, Experience and Education (New York: Macmillan Co., 1938), p. 50.

41. Ibid., p. 177.

42. John Blewett, (Ed.), John Dewey: His Thought and Influence (New York: Fordham University Press, 1960), p. 160.

43. Thelen, Op. Cit., 30.

BIBLIOGRAPHY

Archambault, Reginald D. (ed.), Dewey on Education - Appraisals, New York: Random House, Inc., 1966.

Berstein, Richard J. (ed.), On Experience, Nature and Freedom--Representative Selections, New York: The Liberal Arts Press, Inc., 1960.

Blewett, John (ed.), John Dewey: His thought and Influence, New York: Fordham University Press, 1960.

Bradford, Leland P., Group Dynamics and Education, Washington, D.C.: National Education Association, 1948.

Curtis, Dorothy H. (ed.), Forces in Community Development, Washington, D.C.: NTL-NEA, 1961.

Dewey, John, Democracy and Education, New York: Macmillan, 1916.

Dewey, John, Experiences and Education, New York: Macmillan Company, 1938.

Dewey, John, Human Nature and Conduct, New York: Henry Holt and Company, 1930.

Dewey, John, Reconstruction in Philosophy, New York: Henry Holt and Company, 1930.

Dewey, John, The Quest for Certainty, New York: Minton, Balch, and Company, 1929.

Faculty of the Training Laboratory in Group Development, Group Growth and Educational Dynamics, Washington, D.C.: N.E.A. and Research Center for Group Dynamics, 1948.

Farson, Richard (ed.), *Science and Human Affairs*, Palo Alto: Science and Behavior Books, Inc., 1965.

Geiger, George C., *John Dewey in Perspective*, New York: Oxford University Press, 1958.

Hendel, Charles W. (ed.), *John Dewey and the Experimental Spirit in Philosophy*, New York: The Liberal Arts Press, Inc., 1959.

John Dewey on Education--Selected Writings, New York: Random House, Inc., 1964.

Knowles, Malcolm and Hulda, *Introduction to Group Dynamics*, New York: Association Press, 1959.

Thelen, Herbert A., *Dynamics of Groups at Work*, Chicago: The University of Chicago Press, 1954.

Williams, Robin M., *American Society - A Sociological Interpretation*, New York: Alfred A. Knopf, Inc., 1960.

Winn, Ralph B. (ed.), *John Dewey: Dictionary of Education*, New York: Philosophical Library, 1959.

Worton, Stanley N., *Review Notes and Study Guide to the Major Works of John Dewey*, New York: Monarch Press, Inc., 1964.

CHAPTER THREE

THE VERY IDEA OF A KNOWLEDGE BASE FOR TEACHING

by

C.J.B. Macmillan
Florida State University

Recent developments in educational research assumes a need for a "knowledge base" for teaching. Indeed, the educational community as a whole seems to believe (a) that a knowledge base for teaching is possible, (b) that we are a long way toward having it, and (c) that we're better off with a knowledge-base than without one. All three of these beliefs need examination. That's my task here.

I. AN EXAMINATION OF PEDAGOGICAL REASONING

Let me begin with an example of a teacher in action; I hope that the patterns of reasoning, the appeals to generalized and specific knowledge will be familiar to anyone who has thought seriously about teaching.

Imagine a teacher faced with two young boys in her first grade class; one day, one of them, Albert blows his nose into his fingers and wipes the resultant emission on his rather dirty dungarees. Seeing this, the second, Bobby, does the same thing, wiping his fingers on his rather neat trousers. How is the teacher to deal with such behavior?

The most appropriate thing, one might feel, would be to ignore it entirely; this is merely a feature of the behavior of little boys, something that should not be made too much of. This proposal for (in) action makes assumptions about the normal behavior of little boys, based, perhaps, upon sociological or psychological studies - or perhaps upon the teacher's experience in previous encounters with little boys. It might also be based upon a belief that there are more important things to attend to in the classroom.

But suppose that the teacher believes that one thing that should be taught in her school is appropriate behavior in such circumstances - that they blow their noses into clean tissues and then dispose of the tissues in the wastebasket by the door. This goal might be based upon her knowledge of biology or epidemiology (the spread of germs might lead to some sort of epidemic of colds of flu), or it might be based merely upon her beliefs about what counts as polite behavior for any child - this just isn't done. For whatever reason, she wants to teach these two boys appropriate behavior. What knowledge is relevant as she thinks through such a problem?

She knows this about these two children: Albert comes from a very poor home; it is likely that he has seen this way of blowing one's nose in the family. In such poor families, furthermore, it is unlikely that one would find handkerchiefs or tissues. To teach Albert that his behavior is not appropriate means going against his family's standard behavior. One can assume that she would have learned about such things in her course in educational sociology or anthropology. To teach Albert requires considerable knowledge about such things, as well as knowing Albert personally.

Bobby, on the other hand, comes from a relatively affluent middle-class family; his behavior seems to be a mimicry of Albert. Teaching him requires other sorts of approaches - punishment or some form of shaming him, perhaps. Again, her knowledge of the behavior patterns of certain classes of people is relevant, and is called upon in determining what to do now.

What to do is not given by this knowledge, however, Other theories are called upon as the teacher weighs alternatives. She might believe, for example, that a mere expression of horror ("Ugh! Don't do that!") won't give Albert any options, merely some knowledge of the teacher's weirdness. And acceptance of a family's traditions isn't appropriate for Bobby. How to teach them requires that additional questions be answered: respond loudly in front of the class? take them aside? make a group lesson? etc., etc. An ultimate decision to demonstrate and justify different ways of acting to Albert and to punish Bobby may require different theories - e.g., psychological theories of the impact of different approaches on different types of children, along with some factual discoveries (or decisions, perhaps) about Albert's and Bobby's current knowledge about proper behavior.

It should be clear that the teacher's pattern of thinking is very complex; it involves generalizations from fields as disparate as psychology, sociology, and epidemiology; it involves considerable specific knowledge of the two students; it assumes some concepts of teaching and learning; and it puts these together in a logically complex pattern of deductive and inductive reasoning.

II. SOME COMMENTARY ON THIS EXAMPLE

Let me comment on this example, for it shows some of the elements of pedagogical reasoning that might be relevant to those assumptions about knowledge bases for teaching.

First, this is not an entirely typical example of a teacher dealing with a particular subject matter area - mathematics, history, or language, for example. Rather, it deals with a "behavioral" problem. Nonetheless, it has elements that would be found in most cases of teaching. Specifically, it involves a particular learning goal, viz., the student's learning how to do a particular thing and why (the simplicity of the goal makes it a useful example); it also involves a set of assumptions about the student's background knowledge (which might be stated as questions they ought to ask about the behavior); another set of assumptions about the processes of learning, and still another set about the social background of the situation.

Second, the teacher deals with the boys' behavior in terms of its meaning to them, not merely as a behavior "emitted" by a meaningless robot or mechanism. The teacher must know - or have some good ideas about - the students' minds, and she reacts to that, rather than merely to their conduct. This is very important, especially since some theorists of a behaviorist stamp seem to want to deny the relevance of the meaning of behavior to the agent in their theories of learning and teaching. It is also important because it shows one place in which teachers' ignorance of their students can change everything: the teacher's knowledge must be relevant to the particularities of the subject at hand - the question is "What do they know or believe, or mean, about this particular thing?" not a more generalized "What do they know period?"

Third, the decision about the pedagogical goal could itself be based on different "theoretical" assumptions; her wishing them to use tissues (etc.), it was suggested, might be based upon her belief that it's good manners to behave in such ways, or it might be based upon some theories of good health and the spread of germs. Or it might be an "over-determined" goal - based upon both theories (and even more). What is dangerous here is the room that such "theoretical" differences give for rationalization: her search for a health-justification might be a search merely for a more fashionable justification of what she wants to achieve anyhow. This is the sort of thing that happened (or happens) when scientists searched for - and found - justification for keeping women ignorant, on the grounds that intellectual education would lead to biological harm. There is much room for rationalization, and a necessity for being clear-headed about the real justification for our "educational" goals.

Fourth, the assumption was made (by me) that there are different <u>kinds</u> of knowledge involved in the teacher's decision making procedures. But this is itself an assumption worth examining at considerable depth. What makes one <u>kind</u> of knowledge different from another? Is it the relationship of evidence to conclusion? Is it they type of evidence? Is it something to do with the "objectively reasonable" theory behind the whole thing? For the teacher's decisions may be based upon old wives tales, upon her personal experience of these particular students, or upon theory-laden studies in such academic disciplines as sociology or psychology. Are there grounds for saying that one of these is better than another in teachers' thinking? (This is a problem of the metaphysics or ontology of epistemology, if I understand it correctly: what kind of reality is there in questions of epistemology?)

III. THE VERY IDEA OF A KNOWLEDGE BASE

Now to the main question: is there something recognizable as a "knowledge base" in teaching - something that would help to clarify this example and the myriads of others that might be conjured up? Remember that we began with three (educationists') assumptions: (a) a knowledge base for teaching is possible; (b) we are a long way toward having a knowledge base; and (c) we are better off with a knowledge base than without it. I'll deal primarily with the first of these, for reasons that will become evident.

(a) Is a knowledge base for teaching possible? Well, only if we have some sort of conception of what such a thing might be. But I'm not sure that we do have such a conception - or, even, that such a conception is possible. To show why, I offer the following comments on the problem of defining "knowledge base" in contexts like ours.

Throughout these comments, my assumption is that we are concerned with knowledge of and about teaching; and there may be a further assumption that this in some way will be "theoretical" knowledge rather than "merely" practical knowledge. Such structured knowledge will have elements that would not be found when we merely proceed with teaching without concern for the wider theoretical context of the actions.

There's an underlying metaphor here; presumably we have teaching as the object of concern, and under it - like the base of a statue - some sort of structure on which it "stands." The metaphor has at least two possible interpretations: (a) In the first place, we can imagine the "base" as being something logically and structurally separate from the statue built upon it. The base is one thing, the statue another, and for various reasons, we might search for a different base- the reasons might range from the strength of the support to the aesthetics of the base and statue combined (or separate). If we follow this interpretation of the metaphor, we have two "objects," whose relationship is at best contingent. (b) In a different way, we could think of the base as something that is part of the structure of the statue - the bottom part, perhaps, but nonetheless logically inseparable from the construction as a whole.

If you are building a base for a statue, you don't know how to do it, or what is necessary, if you don't know what the statue will be like; if it's heavy, you need one thing, if light, another; if it's aesthetically of one type, you want or need an aesthetically appropriate base, etc. To follow the metaphor out, an attempt at providing a knowledge base for teaching assumes that we know what teaching is independent of the knowledge base; but surely one task of any theoretical (research?) approach to the development of knowledge about teaching is that of providing an appropriate explication (analysis, definition, etc.) of the central concept. And that concept, as anyone remotely familiar with the literature realizes, is essentially contested. Erotetics anyone? Narrative? Interaction? Freudian relationships?

If the notion of a knowledge base is to be useful, it's important that we be clear which possibility is chosen for distinguishing teaching from its knowledge base. For if the knowledge base is logically separate from teaching, there is a central problem of translation from the base to the statue. Just what is the relationship of the knowledge that underlies teaching and teaching itself? This becomes a central problem for researchers and those who would give advice to teachers - the problem of "bridging," to borrow a term from Fenstermacher.

If, on the other hand, we see the knowledge base as intrinsically related to teaching, then where one begins becomes the problem: do we think that we have to start with the bottom of the statue (so to speak), or that we could begin our constructions at any place in the overall structure? Can we start with the activities of teaching and build out from there? Or do we begin with the things we know about teaching and build upon that structure?

My immediate - and considered - reaction is that there is no adequate way of conceptualizing the relationship between a "knowledge base" and the thing for which it is a base. To see them as logically separate categories, as the statue metaphor suggests, is to miss the ways in which the activities of teaching substantiate knowledge; but to attempt to see the activities and the knowledge as part of the same logical whole may ignore the ways in which separately derived knowledge interacts with the activities.

This may make the other two questions or assumptions otiose. If there are no grounds for saying that there can be a knowledge base, then surely we aren't close to having one. And if there can be no such thing, then we cannot be better off with it than without it.

So what is the fuss all about? Can there be nothing of value here? Is the search for a knowledge base a snipe hunt? Who is left with the bag in the woods?

Part of the problem is that we are trying to define such a notion too tightly. Part of the value of a "programmatic" notion such as "knowledge base" is its vagueness; if it is to attract scholars and others to its cause, the central concepts of a program (or paradigm, or tradition) probably should not be so tightly circumscribed as to scare people away.

But it should be tight enough that one has some sense of the limits and boundaries. We don't want to admit too much witchcraft into our empirical endeavors. But attempting to put any limits upon a notion like "knowledge base," designed to control investigation, may lead us into that snipe hunt. We have an empty bag, and we stand in the forest trying to fill it with a myth.

This much seems clear: We should investigate teaching, we should do it with all of the techniques available to us, and we should continue to attempt to base practice upon the firmest theoretical (and empirical) knowledge we can construct. But we should not assume that we are searching for some identifiable body of knowledge, something whose structure and contents can be determined in advance. It's the search that's important, not some goal that is waiting for us. Designing a knowledge base around the metaphors is like constructing a building with no idea of the purpose of the structure.

Consider the example of that first grade teacher: in her decisions - and the resulting actions - there was considerable use of background knowledge; if she had not known about sociological and psychological theories, it is likely that her actions would have been different. She might have treated both students in precisely the same way, or she might have treated both students with inappropriate punitive techniques. But is it sensible to talk about the (or even her) "knowledge base?" Does it add anything to our description, or is it merely a fancy way of talking, designed to make rather simple relationships into something more complicated?

There is a serious question here for researchers: What ought teachers know in order to be better at their jobs? That question is not the same as "What is the knowledge base for teaching?" The latter suggests another level of discussion, but one that does not add anything to the search or to the practice of teaching.

Harmless jargon-building, one might say - a way of getting us to pull together to engage in the attempt to answer the serious question, i.e., what should teachers know? A slogan whose usefulness can be predicted because it does emphasize the importance of research on teaching. But there may well be real dangers in such a move.

The greatest danger, I suspect, is in those last two assumptions with which we began: assuming that we might be a long way toward a knowledge base for teaching suggests that the search is almost over, or that the goal is in sight. And assuming that we are well off with what we've got enables bureaucrats and others to put limits on the practice of teaching in accord with whatever happens to be the currently fashionable theory of teaching or the currently fashionable "knowledge base." This is the danger, then. Not the search for knowledge about teaching, but the assumption that we are or could be anywhere near having enough knowledge.

If there's any motivation for serious study of things like teaching, it is probably a sense of wonder, a realization that however much we know, there is always more to be learned. If there is to be fruitful and exciting study of teaching, we must accept this - and accepting it means that we cannot afford to believe that we have achieved a final goal, or even that we are likely to reach the end of inquiry. It is essential to keep that sense of wonder alive - both for researchers and for practitioners. The bureaucratic or technician's belief that a knowledge base is already in place allows us to stop searching and merely act.

The very idea of a knowledge base may kill off that essential sense of wonder. That's more harmful, probably, than mere ignorance.

CHAPTER THREE

TEACHER ACCOUNTABILITY FOR STUDENT LEARNING

by

George Newsome
University of Georgia

Teacher accountability for students' learning is not a new idea. It seems to come and go with the changing tide of educational opinion. An educational researcher, Robert M. Travers, has noticed this changing tide of opinion and spoke of it as follows:[1]

> Although educated people in most civilizations, through most of history, have held the belief that the pupil was responsible for learning or not learning, that belief has been abandoned from time to time in favor of the belief that the teacher has much, if not total, responsibility for how much the pupil learns. The 19th century showed one great flirtation with the myth of total teacher responsibility for learning when an effort was made in British schools to fix teacher salaries on the basis of the measured achievement of their pupils. This famous payment-by-results system had devastating effects on British schools and was eventually terminated by Act of Parliament as a result of public outcry.

This same researcher, speaking of some sources of the myth of teacher accountability, has stated:[2]

> One of the sources that contributed to the myth of accountability was the emergence of operant psychology and the idea that the environment totally controlled the pupil's learning. Given that premise, the teacher's task was to provide an environment that would control the pupil's behavior and achieve

specific objectives. The concept of pupil responsibility had no place in the operant psychologist's description of school learning.

What Travers called "operant psychology" is a part of behaviorism. Operant psychology, in conjunction with some more general ideas of behaviorism, and entwined with some ideas of long standing in education, gave rise to what can be called "instructional behaviorism."[3] Unlike some other forms of behaviorism, the central feature of instructional behaviorism is to change or modify behavior by instructional means; namely, by teaching and curriculum. From Edward Lee Thorndike to the present numerous educational psychologists and teacher educators have advocated that there should be specific behavioral objectives for both teaching and curriculum. These objectives were thought to make both curriculum content and teaching procedures explicit to student and educational evaluators. Learning was naively assumed to be measurable changes in behavior as predicted by the objectives.

Instructional behaviorism grew over the decades until it became a generally accepted ideology in education. As it grew it spawned or gave support to performance-based teaching, performance evaluations, teacher accountability, management by objectives, minimum competency testing, and such schemes as planning, programming, and budgeting to achieve objectives. It seems to be the foundation of many of the newer reform programs in education.[4] It seems that reforms, upon close examination, often are found to be "more of the same old things."

Teacher accountability, as part of instructional behaviorism, can be briefly summarized. First, learning is naively assumed to be change or modification of behavior. Second, the purpose of teaching is to change or modify behavior. Third, to insure that what is learned is specifically what was contained in the curriculum and taught by the teacher, the learning or behavior changes must be those stated in the objectives. Fourth, the teacher is accountable for achieving or failing to achieve the stated objectives. This means that the teacher is accountable for the student's learning. It seems as though, to use poor grammar, the teacher must "learn the student."

The purpose of this paper is not to explore the many and varied aspects of teacher accountability, but rather to identify and analyze some very basic arguments which advocates of teacher accountability must use in making a case for accountability. The arguments will be presented in ordinary language, along with their symbolic forms, and their validity or invalidity. The arguments cannot stand alone, so to speak, without contextual backings. Appropriate contextual backings will be discussed and problems will be identified. Finally, an alternative to teacher accountability will be offered.

In order to make a case for teacher accountability that included arguments for it, be they individual arguments, or parts of extended arguments, one would have to use at least one of four basic arguments. For convenience and to avoid unnecessary repetition, these arguments will be labeled A, B, C, and D. In the symbolic forms of the arguments," "T" will be used for "the teacher taught" and "L" for "the student learned." The arguments are presented in Figure 1.

Figure 1

Argument		Logical Form	Validity
A.	If the teacher taught then the student learned	$T \rightarrow L$	Valid by modus
	The teacher taught	T	
	Therefore, the student learned	$\therefore L$	
B.	If the teacher taught then the student learned	$T \rightarrow L$	Fallacy of denial of
	The teacher did not teach	T	the
	Therefore, the student	$\therefore L$	antecedent
C.	If the teacher taught then the student learned	$T \rightarrow L$	Fallacy of affirming
	The student learned	L	the
	Therefore, the teacher taught	$\therefore T$	consequent
D.	If the teacher taught then the student learned	$T \rightarrow L$	Valid by modus
	The student did not learn	$\sim L$	tollens
	Therefore, the teacher did not teach	$\therefore T$	

If the teacher is accountable for the student's learning, then teaching by the teacher implies learning on the part of the student. This is an inescapable premise in any argument for teacher accountability. To be sure, the antecedents and consequents of the argument could be reversed and the second premise changed accordingly, but if that were done, there would be no changes in either the logical forms of the argument or in their validity or invalidity. If the arguments were stated in categorical form, there would be no change in their validity or invalidity.

The first premise is identical in all four arguments. Although it is a statement of implications, it is not clear what kind of implication it is. Four of the more common kinds of implications are represented in the following statements.

1. If A includes B, and B includes C, then A includes C.
2. If an adult male is unmarried, then he is a bachelor.
3. If there is friction, then there will be heat.
4. If it rains, then I will stay at home.

The first statement is a logical implication. The second is a definitional one. The third is a causal implication and the fourth is a decision. In the four arguments under consideration, the first premise is neither logical nor decisional. It, therefore, must be either definitional or causal.

Of the four arguments presented, only A and D are valid ones. It will be assumed that only valid arguments would be used in support of teacher accountability. The major premise of arguments A and D can be interpreted as either definitional or causal. On either interpretation the key words in the arguments are "teacher," "student," and "learned." Being undefined in the arguments, these words could be interpreted in several ways. For example, under what specific conditions can a person be called either a teacher or a student? Under what conditions could one say that the teacher was teaching, as opposed to doing many other things that teachers commonly do, such as grading papers? What is it that is taught? How do we know that it was taught to the student so that the student learned it? What is learning? How do we know that the student learned?

In order to make a convincing case for teacher accountability, the arguments would have to be supported by some sharp distinctions, defensible classifications, precise definitions, and considerable information about teachers, teaching, students, learning, and schooling. Relationships such as those of teaching to learning, teaching to schooling, or schooling to education may require detailed analysis. Arguments are context dependent. They do not stand alone. To make a case is to provide a context with appropriate support or backing for arguments which are a part of the case.

To make a strong case for teacher accountability, one should look beyond the walls of public school buildings. In doing so, one may realize that words like "teacher" and "teaching" are notoriously ambiguous. Parents teach their children, mother bears teach their cubs, craftsmen teach their apprentices, and people teach other people apart from formal schooling. At some time or other, almost everyone will find him[her] self in situations in which he[she] is either teacher or student. The trappings of formal schooling may unduly limit one's views of teachers, teaching, and students.

In either formal schooling or in other life activities, teaching is directly observable. Although teaching activities appear to be obvious, it is difficult to classify them or clearly separate them from activities of the teacher which serve other educational functions. Moreover, teachers and educators in general do not seem to be of one mind about teaching. Teaching has been characterized as guiding and directing inquiry, storing the mind with information, actualizing potential abilities, creating learning environments, intervening or even intruding into the life of students, and modifying behavior. For these and other reasons, there does not seem to be an adequate definition of "teaching" which specifies truly defining characteristics of it.

Like teaching activities, some learning activities are directly observable, but learning itself is not. From observation of students engaged in learning activities, from tests of many kinds, and from more comprehensive evaluations one can infer that learning has or has not occurred. The inference, however, is an inductive one having the liabilities common to inductive inferences.

Because learning must be inductively inferred from observations and data, studies of learning have been largely empirical ones. Empirical studies of learning focus attention upon the learner rather than upon the teacher. Human learners are tremendously complex organisms. Many variables, some of which may not be recognized, enter into human learning. Moreover people are learning all the time. To live is to learn. An adequate account of learning could not be limited to learning from teachers in classrooms. In short, learning is a complex phenomena. There does not seem to be an adequate definition of it.

Given what seems to be known about teaching and learning, our conceptions of them will be both inadequate and debatable. From our limited knowledge, however, it seems that teaching and learning are separate categories of phenomena. Students do learn from teaching and they learn in other ways in the absence of teaching. Teaching and learning are related, but the relationship is a contingent rather than a necessary one.

If the relationship of teaching to learning is a contingent one, then there will be problems concerning the arguments in Figure 1. The first premise in each argument is a statement of implication. It seems to be a necessary rather than a contingent statement. One problem that arises has been called the paradox of material implication.

The concept of material implication in logic does not encompass the full meaning of the four kinds of implication previously discussed. It singles out a common feature of all statements of implication which denies that the antecedent is true and the consequent is false. This feature is shown in the truth table in Figure 2.

Figure 2

P	Q	~Q	P ~Q	~(P~Q)	P → Q
T	T	F	F	T	T
T	F	T	T	F	F
F	T	F	F	T	T
F	F	T	F	T	T

As the truth table illustrates, a denial of the conjunction of P. ~Q is to say that it is not the case that the antecedent is true and the consequent is false, or as shown in column five, not both P and not Q [~ (P. ~ Q)]. The truth table shows that the expression not both P and not Q [~ (P. ~ Q)] is equivalent in meaning and truth value to P implies Q [P -) Q].

The first premise in the argument shown in Figure 1 is: "If the teacher taught, then the student learned." If the teacher taught, but the student did not learn, then the premise would be logically false as shown in the second row of the truth table. The words "taught" and "learned" are key words in the premise. If a teacher teaches a student, the student may or may not learn from the teaching. On the other hand, if the student was taught, then the student learned. "Teach" seems to be a task word, but "taught" is an achievement words. In the same way, "learn" is a task word, but "learned" is an achievement word.

The first premise in the arguments is analytically true by the meaning of the words used in it. It is a definitional implication. Arguments A and D are both valid and analytically sound ones. They are valid and sound however "teaching" and "learning" are defined, because the key words in them are achievement ones. The use of achievement words avoids questions about what was learned, how it was learned, or the quality and amount of the learning. Questions about how teaching and learning are related do not arise. Because arguments A and D are valid and sound by the meanings of the key words in them and by their logical form, they are purely analytic and devoid of substantive content.

The first premise in arguments A and D may also be interpreted as stating a causal relationship. That is, the teacher caused the student to have learned whatever was taught. The truth table for material implication does not, however, provide any empirical information about causal events or their effects. It only shows that __if__ there is a causal relationship, then it fits the __form__ of material implication. For example, if there is friction, then there will be heat. That all cases of friction produce heat would have to be established empirically and not merely by meaning of terms and logical form.

Both friction and heat are empirical phenomena, and they are causally related, but not all empirical phenomena are so related. For example, "If Plato was a philosopher, then Ronald Reagan is President of the United States." Both the antecedent and consequent are empirically true, and the implication would show true in a truth table, simply because true statements imply other true statements. The subject matters are not related empirically, and certainly not by causality. This situation is part of the paradox of material implication.

In arguments A and D one may assume that the teacher was the cause of the student's learning. On the other hand, experience seems to indicate that students do not always learn from the teacher's teaching. The relationship of teaching to learning does not, therefore, seem to be an invariant one, but rather a contingent one. This would be true of tutorials as well as classroom teaching. Teaching is neither a necessary nor a sufficient condition for learning. People learn in many other ways. It seems very unlikely, given the numerous variables that enter into teaching and learning, that a causal relationship could be experimentally demonstrated.

Arguments A and D are valid because the key words in them are achievement words in the past tense. They speak only of cases in which teaching and learning have been successful. Unless these arguments are understood for what they are, their use in cases for teacher accountability for student learning may be more harmful than beneficial to the teaching profession. To expect success in teaching and learning day to day and on all occasions, is to expect too much. Success in teaching and in learning are always matters of degree resulting from effort over time. Learning cannot be mandated.

Teachers work in situations that limit their range of activities. Teachers almost never have the opportunity to set standards for admission to their classes and to recruit students who exceed these standards. They take the students who are assigned to them. They have little control over numerous variables in the school and community that greatly influence students' achievement in schooling. They cannot compensate in their teaching for all of the faults in society that make for poor learning in school. A teacher may teach very well, yet students may not learn what is expected of them.

Teacher accountability for student learning may be an oversimplified idea.[5] It may result in scapegoating teachers for failures in society and education.[6] It does not hold the teacher accountable for teaching or the student accountable for learning. It is misdirected in holding the teacher accountable for the student's learning and holding the student accountable for little beyond attendance. It naively assumes that teachers "learn students." According to an old saying, a person can lead a horse to water, but he cannot make him drink.

Some problems about teacher accountability result from ordinary meanings of "teach" and "taught." For example, dictionaries define "teach" as "to cause to know a subject," "to cause to know how," "to make to know," "to impart knowledge," and "to preach." These older meanings do not fit contemporary teaching practices. Dictionaries also define "teach" as "to guide the studies of." This latter meaning is closer to prevailing practices. The older meanings of "teach" are retained, however, in the belief that teachers can control student learning by control of the classroom environment. The belief that teachers can compel students to learn supports the idea that "if the teacher taught, then the student learned." This belief is falsified daily in the classrooms across the land.

An alternative to teacher accountability is that of teachers' professional responsibilities. Teachers are responsible for mastery of the subject matter they teach. They are responsible for keeping up to date in their teaching fields. It is their responsibility to be aware of the standards for practice in their fields and to practice according to those standards. It is their responsibility to understand the code of professional ethics in teaching and to adhere to it.

Incompetence, malpractice, and violations of the code of ethics are grounds for removing a teacher's certification. Where students are properly and competently taught, but do not learn, the fault is not with the teachers. They may be victims of social conditions, faulty prior education, lack of interest or motivation, or what not. Learning from the curriculum and teaching is on the student's side of the ledger.

FOOTNOTES

1. Robert M. W. Travers, "Myths, Scripts, and Educational Research," *Journal of Research and Development in Education*, 20, 3 (1987), p. 23.

2. Ibid.

3. George L. Newsome, "Instructional Behaviorism: A Critique," *Philosophy of Education 1974: Proceedings of the Philosophy of Education Society*, pp. 336-350.

4. Alan C. Ornstein, "Teacher Accountability: Trends and Policies," *Education and Urban Society*, 18, 2, (1986), pp. 221-229.

5. Ibid.

6. Ibid.

CHAPTER THREE

A METHODOLOGICAL CONSIDERATION IN SOCRATIC DIALOGUE

by

Richard J. Elliott
&
Patricia J. Austin
University of New Orleans

PROLOGUE

It is...commonplace that all research must start from a problem. Research can be successful only if the problem is good; it can be original only if the problem is original. But how can one see a problem, any problem, let alone a good and original problem: For to see a problem is to see something that is hidden. It is to have an intimation of the coherence of hitherto not comprehended particulars. The problem is good if this intimation is true; it is original if no one else can see the possibilities of the comprehension that we are anticipating. To see a problem that will lead to a great discovery is not just to see something hidden, but to see something of which the rest of humanity cannot have even an inkling. All this...commonplace; we take it for granted, without noticing the clash of self-contradiction entailed in it. Yet Plato has pointed out this contradiction in the Meno; He says that to search for the solution of a problem is an absurdity; for either you know what you are looking for, and then there is no problem; or you do not know what you are looking for, and then you cannot expect to find anything (Polanyi, 1966, p. 394).

We could as easily state that all writing must start from a problem and from the above quote, it is easy to assert that the solution of writing problems resides within the students themselves. Prescientific thought places the locus of solution within the individual. Something has to jar that individual, much as in Plato's dialogues Socrates torpifies someone to make him aware that something has gone awry with the reasoning. While Socrates was at home in pursuing diligently the various issues of discussion, he was not that comfortable giving answers to these issues. The strength of his intellect is generally focused on aiding an individual to see for himself certain implausibilities, contradictions, and inconsistencies.

Socrates' generosity in his method is displayed by allowing the individual to detour, revise, and rethink his notions.

In a similar way, students in writing are dealing with ideas that are incomplete, unformed, and undeveloped. Most of students' errors fall into two categories - what they're saying and how they are saying it - meaning and grammar. The Socratic method is surely applicable to one of those categories - what the students are trying to communicate. Teachers of writing have to show that same generosity of spirit as Socrates. In using this method, the teacher helps the students focus on what they are trying to say and ultimately say it. At this juncture, students are no longer defending their notions, but are open to suggestions of how to put their notions across. The strength of the method for the teacher is that it works on the quid and the quale - the what and the how.

While our opening remarks focused on where the solutions of problems lie and the usefulness of the Socratic method in aiding students to solve their problems, it is appropriate to briefly discuss some of the problems in the teaching of writing.

The act of problem-finding is a ...[central] part of general creativity in both the arts and the sciences (Flower & Hayes, 1980, p. 23). Unfortunately, as Berthoff recognized, "a shortcoming of most of our students [is] they do not easily recognize particular problems because they do not have a method for ...formulating critical questions" (1978, p. 4). Good writers according to Flower and Hayes solve a different problem than poor writers. Poor writers "...possess verbal and rhetorical skill which they fail to use because of their underdeveloped image of their rhetorical problem (Flower & Hayes, 1980, p. 23). What Flower and Hayes seem to be saying is that writers do not actually say what they want to say or more often they may have little idea of what it is that they really want to say.

If we recognize that writing is a problem for advanced students and scholars, then we can readily acknowledge how great a problem it must be for beginning students. With the use of dialogue, students ultimately grasp what it is that they are trying to do and then the actual doing of it falls into place. Because writing is personal, feelings are involved.

More sympathetic understanding of those who are participating in the writing process results via the Socratic method. Once the students' ego-concerns are no longer central and their ideas are clear to them, the teacher truly becomes the facilitator and students learn. If teachers can accept the point of view, that the student is or isn't going to do certain things and that they, as teachers, are not going to impose their own thoughts, the process will work. Teachers have to rely on what the students know. This is not unlike normal classroom procedures. When students understand exactly what it is that they are trying to do, the instructional situation works. Socrates in all his dialogues is trying to move someone. Emotions are first strained, the participants are often less than civil, but agreement is reached, and civility eventually prevails, though I am reminded that in some cases this was not so, and Socrates paid the price.

Let us now explore in our own dialogue paralleling the Meno, a teacher's bantering with Socrates the notions of teaching writing and making better writers. What will hopefully emerge from the dialogue is a representation of how one teacher is jarred to reexamine and redefine her own methodological questions.

DIALOGUE

Ms. A: Can you tell me, Socrates, is writing something that can be taught by direct instruction? Or does it come merely by practice? Or is it neither through teaching nor practice but through natural aptitude or through development that a person becomes a better writer? It seems that no matter what I do, some students write interesting stories and others write stories that are so dreadfully dull.

Socrates: Well, Ms. Austin your professors in the Department of Education may have gotten you into the habit of expecting an answer for any question you might ask just as they themselves invite questions of every kind and never fail to answer them, but here there is a dearth of wisdom. Ask a question among philosophers and they will all alike laugh and say, "You must think I am singularly fortunate to know whether writing can be taught or how it is acquired." The fact is that far from knowing whether it can be taught, I have no idea what you mean by writing. And how can I know a property of something when I don't even know what it is?

Ms. A: True, writing is regarded as different things. Following the current writing research, I'm referring to the process of writing itself rather than to the written product.

Socrates: It does appear that a discussion of the process of writing logically precedes a discussion of the product, yet I am troubled. I don't know how to proceed. Therefore, humor me a little. What do you mean by the process of writing?

Ms. A: Writing, according to Flower and Hayes (1983), is a recursive process in which the writer orchestrates three subprocesses--planning, translating, and reviewing. Other researchers call these subprocesses or phases prewriting, writing, and rewriting; still others call them rehearsing, drafting, and revising. Researchers usually label them and discuss them in sequential order, but the phases don't necessarily occur in that order. I think you'll see what I mean when I describe what happens when people write. During the planning phase, writers do just that--plan what's coming next. They may plan by daydreaming, jotting notes, or even by writing a whole first draft to discover what it was that they wanted to say to begin with. Once writers have planned, they translate thoughts into words. They actually write or draft so that the plan becomes a text....

Socrates: Now wait. Aren't you contradicting yourself? In the translation phase, if writers translate thoughts into words, then can we not say that planning had to come first? And then is the writing process truly recursive?

Ms. A: Well, I think that in the model of the process of writing that Flower and Hayes (1983) posed, planning usually comes first, but it doesn't come only at that point.

Socrates: Usually?

Ms. A: Yes, usually.

Socrates: I wonder, would you be satisfied to say that a student knows what a square is if he says that it usually has four sides?

83

Ms. A: No.

Socrates: Then why is it that you seem satisfied to say that you know what the process of writing is if you know what it usually is?

Ms. A: Now you're trying to compare things that are completely different. Mathematics is more concrete than writing. The model of the writing process that Flower and Hayes posited was a model of good writers and yes, good writers usually have some plan of what they're going to write before they write it.

Socrates: Enough said--we shall not argue the point. I'm more interested in what you said about the process of writing as the model of good writers. Exactly what does that mean? If I am not a good writer, do I write differently?

Ms. A: Yes, in a way. What happens with some writers is that they simply write. There is no forethought, no reflection--little or no planning or reviewing. They just write. Sometimes what they write is almost nonsense. Nothing follows logically; there are great gaps in what they say. Yet they don't look back over what they wrote and don't realize that they haven't made sense unless someone (like a teacher) points it out to them. Other writers make sense, but their writing isn't elaborated. They just don't realize that what they've written could be so much better if only they would reread, rethink, revise, and rewrite.

Socrates: Ah, we seem to have come now to a different question--whether or not we can make someone better. We never did decide if writing could be taught, but let us assume for the moment that it can be. If writing can be taught, then it can be improved. Indulge me a while longer. We do know that writing is another form of communicating so let us consider now different ways of communicating. When a baby is hungry, it cries. Is it not better to him that someone understand his message so that he will be fed?

Ms. A: Yes of course.

Socrates: If you are driving and you begin to change lanes in heavy traffic, is it not better to you that you understand the message when someone lays on his horn?

Ms. A: Yes, certainly, Socrates, but I'm afraid I fail to see the....

Socrates: Then when a writer intends to communicate any message, is it not better to him that his intended message be understood by the reader?

Ms. A: Yes.

Socrates: Think again now of our crying baby. If he whimpers for hours and no one feeds him, has he conveyed a "hungry" cry?

Ms. A: No, I suppose not.

Socrates: Yet if he wails for only five minutes and someone feeds him, would you not say he has conveyed a "hungry" cry?

Ms. A: I would.

Socrates: And if you in your car hear a polite little honk as you begin to change lanes and end up a corpse, you never would be able to say that the other driver just didn't convey his message.

Ms. A: This is true.

Socrates: Then would you agree that writing is better writing if it communicates its intended message than writing that does not?

Ms. A: Yes, that makes sense.

Socrates: Then that brings us to reconsider how we arrive at good writing. At the beginning of this discussion, you dismissed the product of writing to focus on the writing process. Is it really possible to separate the process of writing from the written product? Further, is it even possible to talk about the writing process and the written product in the absence of the writer?

Ms. A: It seems to me, Socrates, that you have indeed caught me. At the beginning of our discussion I felt sure that we could talk about just the writing process. Now I see that the product of the writing is equally important. When the intentions of the writer are satisfied, then through the process, the writer will have achieved a better product.

Socrates: And it seems to me, Ms. Austin, that you have come a long way in considering the problem of method. Perhaps now we can return to consider your original question--can writing be taught and if so how?

Ms. A: Another time, Socrates, at the moment I'm already late for recess duty.

EPILOGUE

There are two problems that teachers face with method in the course of instruction, one is understanding the method and the other is practicing the method. Clearly, Socrates had an understanding of his own method, whether complete or incomplete as some have claimed (Vlastos).

The Socratic method we suggest is complete since it aids a student to say more clearly what he wishes to say and to realize that what is being said is reasonably correct. In Platonic dialogue, Socrates goes through propositions of establishing premises but formally falls short of true inductions. From our vantage point, Socrates seems to be aware of this; he does not talk perfectly as to his conclusions in the form of a disjunction [not P or not S .... More appropriately he states--according to this....] This lack of formal logic is not important to the method. The purpose of the method is more modest--aiding students to perceive relationships among propositions. The beauty of Socrates' method is that he does not assume certainty about the truth or falsehood of any one proposition, slipping easily out of one set of conclusions and into others.

The second problem in instruction is practicing the method. One is faced with what is the method trying to do. One does not have to read into the dialogue too far to realize what Socrates is not trying to do. He is not trying to say what is true, and what is not true, or trying to prove another false. Emerging from the dialogue is a discussion of whether one can be committed to what is being stated. Are there indeed reasonable relationships between propositions and are there warranties to certain assertions? It is not our purpose to go into a detailed analysis of the Socratic method, but a teacher who uses the method, should be aware that the practice of the method is essential to its success.

The teacher of writing is faced with the same two problems--understanding the method and practicing the method. The Socratic method implies that the role of the teacher is not to convey knowledge to the student but to jar the student's thinking; not to impose his own opinions and beliefs but to elicit those of the student; not to direct the writer to write what he thinks the teacher wants him to write, but to lead the writer to define and clarify his own meaning. In applying the method, the teacher must be comfortable with the state of ambiguity which seems to prevail, acknowledging that in dialogue, response cannot be controlled. In practicing the method, hopefully teachers will lead poor writers to do what good writers naturally do--think, write, rethink, rewrite--to evolve and communicate a thought or problem that is worth communicating, and they will lead good writers not to give up too soon. If in the teaching of writing, the students are able to discriminate between the important and unimportant and they are successful in communicating this, are they not better for the exercise?

REFERENCES

Berthoff, A.E. (1978) "Towards a pedagogy of knowing," Freshman English News, 7, 4.

Emig, J.A. (1971) The composing processes of twelfth graders (Research report no. 13) Urbana, Illinois: National Council of Teachers of English.

Flower, L.S. and Hayes, J.R. (1983) "Uncovering cognitive processes in writing: An introduction to protocol analysis" (pp. 206-219). In Mosenthal, P., Tamor, L. and Walmsley, S.S., (Eds.) Research on writing: Principles and methods. New York: Longman, Inc.

Flower, L.S. and Hayes, J.R. (1980) "The cognition of discovery: Defining a rhetorical problem," College Composition and Communication, 31, 21-32.

Graves, D.H. (1973) Children's writing: Research directions and hypotheses based upon an examination of the writing processes of seven-year-old children. (Doctoral dissertation, The State University of New York at Buffalo). Dissertation Abstracts International, 34, 6255A.

Plato, Meno, trans. Jowett, B. (1953) The dialogues of Plato Vol. 1. pp. 249-301. Oxford: Clarendon Press.

Polanyi, M. (1966) "Tacit knowing." In Buford, T.O. (Ed.) Toward a philosophy of education (pp. 382-396). New York: Holt, Rinehart and Winston, Inc.

Vlastos, G. in Plato, Protagoras B. Jowett's trans. extensively revised by Ostwald, M. (1956) edited with an introduction by Vlastos, G. Indianapolis: The Bobbs-Merrill Company, Inc.

CHAPTER THREE

TEACHER SUBJECT MASTERY TESTING: A PARTIAL ALTERNATIVE TO TEACHER EVALUATION

by

Carolyn Lavely
&
John Follman
University of South Florida

There have been many journal articles devoted to evaluation of public school teachers in general, and career ladder and merit pay in particular. Lieberman (1985) advocated educational specialty boards as a means of nationalizing merit pay. His analogies for educational specialty boards are national boards in medicine and also an accounting examination coordinated, with national level cut-off scores. The state of Nevada created an autonomous teacher licensure board, the first autonomous panel established in a decade, with the authority to set licensure and recertification requirements for teachers and other educational personnel (Rodman, 1987). (For excellent overview of teacher testing in the several states, now some 48 in all, see Rudner, 1987).

The purpose of this paper is to articulate a partial alternative to contemporary approaches to teacher evaluation. This alternative is increased pay for teachers who demonstrate mastery of content knowledge, as in merit pay and/or career ladder systems. We advocate this approach because of the problems explicit in the evaluation of teacher performance. Some of these problems are iterated below.

One problem in teacher evaluation is the crucial teacher evaluation median correlation (r) of .43 between students' achievement test scores and their ratings of the teaching effectiveness of their instructor (Follman, 1974; Cohen, 1981). This is a problem because only 18.49% of the variance is jointly associated with student ratings of teacher effectiveness and student achievement, the most important measure of effectiveness of teaching.

The r's between teachers' subject matter knowledge scores on standardized achievement tests, such as the

National Teacher Examinations (NTE), and observations of their classroom teaching performance, usually have been .30 or less (Quirk, Witten & Weinberg, 1972).

Airasian & Madaus (1983) observed that correlations between multiple choice standardized examinations and more direct measures of instructional outcomes are seldom high. The r's between other teacher presage variables and students' achievement scores are also very low. Only teacher verbal ability, clarity, etc. (Coleman, et al. 1966; Rosenshine & Furst, 1971), and also teacher enthusiasm correlate with student achievement and then usually only modestly and inconsistently.

The correlations of the ratings of teacher effectiveness between the different pairs of criterion groups, students, teachers (selves), peers, and administrators are low except for peers and administrators, mdn. r= .69, and for peers and students, mdn. r= .49 (Follman, March 1, 1985).

Unreliability of administrators' ratings of teaching effectiveness, sometimes because of a lack of variance as when administrators rate everyone high, which they often do, as do others, i.e., officers rating military fitness reports. Medley & Coker (1987, b) note that the literature of the validity of principals' judgements of teaching effectiveness shows consistently negative findings. In their investigation of principals' judgements of teachers' effectiveness in performing three central teaching roles the overall mean correlations for grades 2, 3, 4, 5, and 6, respectively were .12, .24, .10, .23, .18, and .17. Medley & Coker further concluded that no amount of training will change principals' overall impressions of their teachers' teaching effectiveness. In another analysis of the same data, Medley & Coker (1978, a) found that principals viewed the teachers in their own respective schools as far superior to teachers in other schools. they concluded that the most important finding in that study was the low accuracy of the average principal's judgement of teachers' teaching performances.

The 18 comparable competencies of the high inference Teaching Performance Assessment Instruments (TPAI) and also of the low inference Classroom Observations Keyed for Effectiveness Research (COKER) correlate very low, reflecting the instrument dependent nature of the criterion variable (Dickson & Wiersma, 1982).

Pre-service and in-service teachers do not receive similar levels of ratings of effectiveness of teaching (Dickson, Wiersma & Jurs, 1984). The correlation between pre-service and in-service teachers on teaching effectiveness, the same instrument, i.e., TPAI, is very low. Different types of raters, i.e., raters (professors) of pre-service teachers vs. raters (public school teachers and/or administrators) of in-service teachers, apparently rate on different criteria.

Why are these r's with the criterion so low? We content that the major reason lies in the criterion, i.e., evaluation of the teaching, especially of the teaching process.

We believe that these r's are unlikely to be found to be higher in the foreseeable future, if ever, since we believe they reflect the serious underlying criterion problem, not some measurement or statistical artifact that can be remedied.

FLORIDA APPROACH

Since the criterion problem is unlikely to be resolved in the foreseeable future we have been taking a different approach in Florida, i.e., the teacher career ladder. It involves substantial testing.

We advocate that rewarding teachers who know more subject matter than other teachers, is not only doable but actually affords more knowledgeable teachers an opportunity for a financial incentive just like the opportunities available to professionals in medicine, law, accounting, etc., opportunities which exist in part because of their high test scores on MCAT, LSAT, etc.

It is noted here that the criterion research, limited in quantity that is in disciplines other than education, i.e., medicine, law, accounting, etc., in which such career related decisions as admission, scholarships, hiring, placement, licensing, etc., also demonstrates the same, low level correlations between test scores and the on-the-job criteria which characterize the education criterion research documented above. Therefore, we argue that educators should have the same kind of opportunities for rewards as doctors, lawyers, accountants, etc., and should not be discriminated against because of the large volume of low correlation predictor-criterion research. Incidentally this volume of research is so large that it far transcends the total of predictor-criterion research across the disciplines of medicine, law, accounting, dentistry, etc., combined.

GENERAL ARGUMENTS FOR TESTING TEACHERS

Several general arguments for testing teachers will be presented.

One argument is that in the knowledge enterprise, i.e., education, it is entirely appropriate to pay an incentive to those teachers who demonstrate superior subject matter knowledge. This incentive can serve either as a temporary expedient while we prepare full scale professional evaluation, through national certification such as that suggested by Lieberman (1985) and affirmed by Shanker (1985,a), or through local level administration, or continued as a part of a total incentive package, which might include pre-service tuition write-offs, competitive starting salaries, higher salaries, merit pay, career ladders, etc.

We note that teachers' salaries nationally have risen 30% over the last five years. Assuming for the next few years that salaries continue to increase at about a 6-7% rate, and that inflation remains at half or less of the increase, we believe that teachers will become more amenable to being tested in merit pay, career ladder, differentiated staffing types of programs, especially if participation in the programs is voluntary and for additional money, as is contemplated. We note that teachers in Rochester, New York reached a contract which will ultimately pay teachers, specifically lead teachers in a career ladder type of program, as much as $70,000 per year (Rodman, September 9, 1987).

Also, in a 1984 survey, 82% of responding teachers said that they either "agreed" or "tended to agree" with recommendations from national and state committees calling for career ladders for teachers, as did 92% of principals (<u>Education Week</u>, September 26, 1984).

We advocate that teacher evaluation be shifted from the current artificial inductive basis to a rational, deductive basis. Our main argument is that the current purported inductive approach is inadequate because of the criterion problem which we believe will not be resolved soon, if ever.

Haberman (1986) articulate six conditions for awarding teaching licenses. Testing is heavily implicated in all six. As Haberman observed, we have to stop criticizing tests of teaching because they lack predictive validity and recognize that other professionals realize that test items assess knowledge, not practice.

Ebel (1975) argued that excellence in education was excellence in learning and that excellence in learning was mainly verbal knowledge and that verbal knowledge was the chief ingredient in human wisdom, even the principal basis of human virtue. Ebel further argued that cognitive competence was a necessary but not sufficient condition for classroom effectiveness and, because of its vital importance and because it can be measured, it should be measured in licensing, employing, and promoting teachers. Teachers cognitive competence was viewed by Ebel (1977) as what was to be taught, how it should be taught, and also how to help students with personal, social, and emotional problems that impeded their learning.

Darling-Hammond (1986,a) noted that there are two important functions of tests, i.e., screening, and defining the professional knowledge base for a practitioner.

Ebel (1977) argued that the NTE was not purported to predict teacher success in the classroom but that it would indicate how much the person knew about the job of teaching. In another article, Ebel (1975) indicated that the test is as good a criterion of competence to teach "as we are likely to get."

Peterson (1987) described a contemporary teacher evaluation system in three Utah school districts involving optional use of the NTE along with other evidence in the promotion process of eligible experienced teachers.

For an update on the NTE, especially its devastating impact on minority teachers, see Anrig Baratz-Snowden & Goertz (1987). Also, see Hackley

(1985) for a description of a teacher training program designed to meet this problem.

Shanker (October 10, 1985) articulated a scenario in which in the following eight years there will not be enough teachers, one estimate being 1.65 million needed additional teachers, and argued that there will be some kind of role differentiation. In the differentiation of these roles, tested teacher subject matter knowledge will necessarily have to be one criterion.

Shulman (1986) concluded that professional examinations for teachers must be developed. These examinations must measure both content and process including content structures and pedagogical knowledge of both general and specialized curricular knowledge.

The Rand report recommended that states should license teachers only after they have completed a supervised internship and passed a rigorous examination which evaluates their ability to teach (Rodman, November 6, 1986).

Shanker (1985,b) advocated a tough national teacher examination consisting of appropriate subject matter, ability to make judgements, justifications for instructional decisions, and successful completion of an internship program.

Pipho (1986) concluded that testing of teachers both initial, and practicing, may have become the centerpiece of the contemporary raising of standards for teachers.

Popham & Kirby (1987) argued that every child in the public schools has the right to be taught by a literate teacher and that the purpose of teacher recertification tests is to ensure that teachers are at least literate. Prerequisite to this concern about teacher literacy or lack thereof is the assertion of Senator George McGovern that one-third of Florida teaching applicants in 1976 failed an eight-grade general knowledge test (Phi Delta Kappan, 1979). Also see Rudner (1987).

ARGUMENTS IN BEHALF OF TESTED TEACHER SUBJECT MATTER KNOWLEDGE

Following are some of the deductive arguments in behalf of tested teacher knowledge as one criterion of teacher effectiveness.

One argument is that teacher subject matter knowledge is a necessary condition for effective teaching. We do not argue that subject matter knowledge is a sufficient condition for effective teaching.

Stephens (1967) developed a thoughtful analysis of the relationship between teacher knowledge and student learning. His analysis encompassed both inductive and deductive aspects. Stephens' inductive interpretation was that the data are most confusing and it was difficult to point out any systematic trends. Stephens' deductive analysis was that the teacher must have some knowledge of the subject.

Lorite (1977) noted that current trends include a greater emphasis on cognitive mastery by teachers.

Marx & Winne (undated) argued that teachers must have subject matter knowledge.

Schon (1983) characterized teachers as technical experts who impart privileged [sic] knowledge to students.

The quintessential lay, and also professional educator, position about teacher testing was proposed by Medley (1984) who asserted that "the belief that teachers should know what it is they are supposed to teach is so strong that we may expect subject-matter tests to be a part of any teacher testing program."

Shulman (1985) is involved in a research program of the study of knowledge in teaching in part through examination of novice vs. expert teachers. In an early effort in this project he addressed the issue of content knowledge in teaching noting that content knowledge alone will not suffice but that neither will any conception of teaching quality that ignores the central role of content knowledge.

Pipho (1986) in an analysis of educational reform in the states, concluded that teacher testing, both for initial certification and also for practicing teachers, is not going to go away and may in fact become the centerpiece of the effort to raise standards for teachers. We submit that, if as projected, half of the public school teaching force leaves in the next six years and has to be replaced, entry level testing, as the most objective, reliable and perhaps valid criterion, will be the centerpiece of teacher entry.

The Carnegie Forum on Education and the Economy Task Force has recommended establishment of a national certification board of teachers. As part of this process the Teacher Assessment Project at Stanford University has received an $817,000 grant from the Carnegie Corporation to develop two model teacher assessments (Haertel, 1987). One of these is teaching fractions to elementary students and the other is teaching history of the American Revolution to secondary students. We view these foci as narrow.

The contrary position to the advocacy of testing teachers was articulated by Madaus & Pullin (1987) who asserted that teacher certification generic tests have a serious validity problems part of which is the narrow range of items, mostly educational psychology, included therein.

DEFINITIONS OF TEACHING CONTENT KNOWLEDGE

Professor Denison Olmstead (1845) of Yale College characterized the virtues of the perfect teacher as knowledge of the subject, knowledge of kindred subjects, intellectual qualities, moral qualities, refined manners, and knowledge of the world, as far back as 1845. The critical role of testing in determining knowledge of the subject, knowledge of kindred subjects, intellectual qualities, and also knowledge of the world, is manifestly clear.

Elbaz (1981) argued that the most likely approach to understand the teacher's role is teachers' knowledge. Elbaz then categorized teachers' knowledge into five categories; subject matter, curriculum, practical, personal, and interaction.

Jackson (1986) articulated three approaches to the definition of teaching, generic, epistemic, and consensual. The generic definition requires that there is an important difference between a definition of teaching and the performance of teaching. An epistemic definition links the teaching activity to the concept of knowledge propounded by most modern epistemologists. A consensual definition is similar to the epistemic but more flexible while attempting to distinguish between ways of teaching which are standard and those which are nonstandard.

Gifford (1987) in Rudner (1987) advocated that a new teacher test should be designed measuring: subject matter competency; knowledge of learning theory; ability to monitor student progress; create well balanced lessons; and evaluate student progress.

Rudner (1987) observed that most teacher certification tests assess the same content, i.e., communication skills, general knowledge, and professional knowledge.

Shulman (1986) defined three kinds of teaching content. One kind of content is the amount and organization of knowledge per se. Ways cited by Shulman to characterize content knowledge include Bloom's cognitive taxonomy, Gagne's varieties of learning, Schwab's distinction between substantive and syntactic structures of knowledge, and Peter's notions that parallel Schwab's. The second kind is pedagogical content knowledge with the emphasis on the particular form of subject matter knowledge that embodies the aspects of content most germane to its teachability. The third is curricular knowledge.

Shulman (1986) suggested three forms of teacher knowledge; propositional, case, and strategic. Propositional knowledge was categorized into principles, maxims, and norms. Cases were categorized into prototypes, precedents, and parables.

Shulman (1986) also argued that evaluation of teachers in most states purported to be "research-based" ignores the subject matter, what he and his colleagues characterize as the "missing paradigm." The "research-based," pedagogical, perception emphasizes such notions as direct instruction, time on task, wait time, ordered turns, lower-order questions, etc. Shulman noted that a century ago the defining characteristic of pedagogy was knowledge of content. Missing today is treatment of the content taught including questions asked and explanations offered.

Shulman and Sykes (1986), cited in Tamir (1987), defined the knowledge base of teaching as "that body of understanding and skill, of dispositions and values, of character and performance that together underlie the capacity to teach." They listed eight categories which encompass this base:

1. General/liberal education including basic skills of reading, math, writing, and reasoning.
2. Content knowledge in the domains in which teaching occur.
3. Content-specific pedagogical knowledge.
4. General knowledge of pedagogical principles and practice.
5. Curricular knowledge.
6. Understanding of student diversity and individual differences.
7. Performance skills (including voice, manner, poise).
8. Foundations of professional understanding (including history and policy; philosophy and psychology; cultural and cross-cultural factors and professional ethics).

Shulman (1987) described the prototypes of teacher assessment he and colleagues are developing. They decided that teacher assessment should consist of at least four components, i.e., written assessments, assessment center exercises, documentation of performance during supervised field experiences, and direct observation of practice by trained observers. They are currently developing teacher assessment protocols in elementary arithmetic, i.e., fractions, and in secondary social studies, i.e., a unit on the American Revolution and the formation of government. Planned are units on the assessment of literacy (elementary), and also in biology (secondary).

Tamir (1987) then articulated a framework for teachers' knowledge consisting of: general education; personal performance; subject matter; general pedagogical; subject matter specific pedagogical; and foundations of the teaching profession.

Smith & Neale (1987) taxonomized teacher knowledge in science into: substantive subject matter knowledge; pedagogical content knowledge; teacher knowledge of typical student errors and the usual development path that student progress takes; and knowledge of particular effective teaching strategies.

Feiman-Nemser & Floden (1986) observed that researchers have portrayed teachers' knowledge as a mixture of idiosyncratic experience and personal synthesis. They quoted Elbaz who suggested five types of practical knowledge in teaching: self; teaching milieu; subject matter; curriculum development; and instruction.

Hawley (1986) argued that, in order to enter teaching internship, candidates would have to demonstrate college-level communication and computation skills, as well as thorough knowledge of their subject matter.

Darling-Hammond (1986,b) overviewed teacher tests and concluded that the knowledge tested by them is: recognition of facts within subject areas; knowledge of school law and bureaucratic procedures; and recognition of the "correct" teaching behavior described in a short scenario. She criticized current tests as being too limited, narrow, superficial, easy, and technique oriented.

SUBJECT MATTER TEST TABLE OF SPECIFICATIONS

One of the earliest taxonomies of teaching activities was reported by Charters, Waples & Capen (1929). From a variety of sources including previous investigators, professional literature, department heads, deans of colleges of education, and 6,054 teachers, a grand total of 236,655 teaching activities, including duplicates was obtained. Seven main classifications were created: classroom instruction; school and class management; supervision of pupils' extra-classroom activities; relationship with school personnel; relationships with members of school community; professional and personal advancement; and school plant and supplies.

Specifications in the 1940 NTE test were: Intellectual and Communicative Skills 30%; Cultural and Contemporary Background 40%; and Professional Information 30% (Wilson, 1986). Wilson noted that ETS officials stressed that the exams did not measure the totality of teaching ability and that they should not be judged by their correlation with "available criteria" of teaching ability. In the 1980s the test composition is: Communication skills, 115 multiple choice items and one essay; General Knowledge, 120 multiple choice; and Professional Knowledge, four sets of 35 multiple choice items, three of which (sets) are scored. Wilson concluded from her historical overview that there has been continuity of test content and justification, that logical or content validity was primary, and that there is a paradoxical relationship between the tests and teacher education curricula.

Goodfellow factor analyzed 97 ratings of importance to teacher job success of tasks. Eight factors were identified: classroom teaching; student-teacher interaction; supervision; teacher-parent relationships; extracurricular activities; record keeping; professional development/interaction; and lesson preparation.

Pugach & Raths (1983) concluded that at least five domains of teacher assessment can be directed: basic academic skills; general knowledge; specific content knowledge; professional knowledge and skills; and on-the-job performance.

In 1984, Connecticut, for its beginning teacher support program, validated a set of generic teaching competencies against seven other systems' set of developed generic teaching competencies, i.e., Arizona, Florida, Georgia, Maryland, South Carolina, Virginia, and Dade County, Florida (Streifer, 1987). Five broad Connecticut set constructs, planning, instruction, formal student evaluation, professional knowledge [demonstrates knowledge of subject matter], and professional responsibilities, were validated empirically, while two professional knowledge constructs, (demonstrates knowledge of applied learning psychology, and demonstrates knowledge of school law) were not.

Medley (1984) argued that there are two kinds of knowledge that teachers need, academic knowledge and clinical knowledge.

Shulman (1986) noted that professional board examinations would test: knowledge of general pedagogy; learners and their backgrounds; principles of school organization, finance, and management; historical, social, and cultural foundations of education; teaching performance; and other areas.

The *Florida Performance Measurement System* (FPMS) recognizes the importance of teacher subject matter knowledge, i.e., conceptual, causal, value, and fundamental rules (Smith and Peterson, January 31, 1986). They also observed that a teacher cannot teach these knowledge without command of them.

For a contemporary teacher job analysis see Rosenfeld, Thornton & Skurnik (1986) who conducted a job analysis of teaching to underpin the structure of the NTE. In one statistical analysis 341 teachers from Georgia and 341 teachers from New Jersey made importance ratings of 83 job tasks. The ratings were factor analyzed (principal components) which resulted in a six factor solution of core job functions: managing and influencing student behavior; clerical, administrative, and other professional functions; assessing, grading and recording student learning progress and evaluating instructional effectiveness; planning the lessons, selecting the materials, and previewing the instructional program; implementing the planned instructional program using a variety of approaches; and identifying students with individual or similar instructional needs and teaching them accordingly. There was overall agreement among both the teachers and the experts that 57 of the 59 knowledge areas were important both for entry into the teaching profession and also for important teacher core tasks or duties. There is also an extensive iteration of relevant researches.

RECOMMENDATIONS

As Chang (1985) observed, the pre-condition for attainment of all these teaching levels is testing.

In the meantime, while research on teacher evaluation continues, we recommend that teacher evaluation be justified on a deductive, not inductive, basis and then conducted on a componential basis of which tests would be one component. Test components would include: experience; pedagogy; subject matter mastery. Testing would be required at the following levels: entry-competencies; certification, recertification, alternate certification; merit pay; career ladder rungs; and national educational specialty boards.

REFERENCES

Airasian, P.W. & Madaus, G.T. "Linking testing and instruction: Policy issues," Journal of Educational Measurement, 20, 103-118.

Arnig, G.R. (1986) "Standing fast," Phi Delta Kappan, 67, 771-772.

Arnig, G.R., Baratz-Snowden, J., & Goertz, M.E. (1987) "Testing policies and minority participation in teaching: A look at the research." American Educational Research Association, Washington, D.C.

Chang, M.K. (1985) "Quality control in teacher education," Scholar and Educator, 9, 70-74.

Charters, W.W., Waples, D., & Capen, S.P. (1929) "The Commonwealth teacher-training study." Chicago, Illinois: The University of Chicago Press.

Cohen, P.A. (1981) "Student ratings of instruction and student achievement: A meta-analysis of multisection validity studies," Review of Educational Research, 51, 281-309.

Coleman, J.S., Campbell, E., Hobson, C., McPartland, J., Mood, A., Weinfield, F., & York, R. (1966) Equality of educational opportunity. Washington, D.C.: U.S. Department of Health, Education, and Welfare.

Darling-Hammond, L. (1986,a) "Raising professional standards and teacher quality." American Educational Research Association.

Darling-Hammond, L. (1986,b) "Teaching knowledge: How do we test it?" American Educator, 46, 18-21.

Ebel, R. L. (1975) "The use of tests in educational licensing, employment, and promotion," Education and Urban Society, 8, 1, 19-32.

Ebel, R. L. (1977) "Comments on some problems of employment testing," Personnel Psychology, 30, 55-63.

Education Week, (September 26, 1984) "Principals, teachers endorse career ladders in a survey." 4.

Elbaz, F. (1981) "The teacher's 'practical knowledge': Report of a case study," Curriculum Inquiry, 11, 43-71.

Feiman-Nemser, S. & Floden, R. E. (1985) "The cultures of teaching" in Handbook of Research in Teaching, Third edition, edited by Merlin C. Wittrock. New York: Macmillan Publishing Company.

Follman, J. (March 1, 1985) "Weight allocation models of criteria of teacher effectiveness." American Association of School Administrators, Dallas, Texas.

Haberman, M. (1986) "Licensing teachers: Lessons from other professions," Phi Delta Kappan, 67, 719-722.

Hackley, L. V. (1985) "The decline in the number of black teachers can be reversed," Educational Measurement: Issues and Practices, 4, 17-19.

Haertel, E. H. (1987) "Toward a national board of teaching standards: The Stanford teacher assessment project," Educational Measurement: Issues and Practices, 6, 23-24.

Hawley, W. D. (1986) "Toward a comprehensive strategy for addressing the teacher shortage," Phi Delta Kappan, 67, 712-718.

Jackson, P. (1986) The practice of teaching. New York: Teachers College, Columbia University.

Lieberman, M. (1985) "Educational specialty boards: A way out of the merit pay morass," Phi Delta Kappan, 67, 103-107.

Linn, R. L. (1986) "Educational testing and assessment," American Psychologist, 41, 1153-1160.

Lortie, D. C. (1977) "The balance of control and autonomy in elementary school teaching," in Educational Organization and Administration. Edited by D. A. Erickson. Berkeley, California: McCutchan Publishing Corporation.

Madaus, G. F. & Pullin, D. (1987) "Teacher certification tests: Do they really measure what we need to know?" Phi Delta Kappan, 69, 31-38.

Marx, R.W., Winne, P. H. (undated) "The shape of teaching to come: Implications for the national teacher examination." National Teacher Examinations Policy Council.

Medley, D. M. (1984) "A valid teacher competency test: Is such a thing possible?" Journal of Human Behavior and Learning, 1, 1-5.

Medley, D. M., & Coker, H. (1987,a) "How valid are principals' judgements of teacher effectiveness? Phi Delta Kappan, 69, 138-140.

Medley, D. M., & Coker, H. (1987,b) "The accuracy of principals' judgements of teacher performance," Journal of Educational Research, 80, 242-247.

Olmstead, D. (1845) "Lecture III on the Sean Ideal of the perfect teacher." American Institute of Instruction. Boston, 15, 83-109.

Peterson, K. D. (1987) "Use of standardized tests in teacher evaluation for career ladder systems," Educational Measurement: Issues and Practices, 6, 19-22.

Phi Delta Kappan, (1987) " 'Intolerable' literacy rate blasted by Senator McGovern," 60, 341.

Pipho, C. (1986) "States move reform closer to reality," Phi Delta Kappan, 68, K 1-8.

Popham, W. J., & Kirby, W. N. (1987) "Recertification tests for teachers: A defensible safeguard for safety," Phi Delta Kappan, 69, 45-49.

Pugach, M. C., & Raths, J. D. (1983) "Testing teachers: Analysis and recommendations," Journal of Teacher Education, 34, 37-43.

Quirk, T. J., Witten, B. J., and Weinberg, S. F. (1972) "Review of studies of the concurrent and predictive validity of the National Teacher Examinations," Review of Educational Research, 43, 647-662.

Rodman, B. (November 26, 1986) "Rand Corporation drafts comprehensive teacher-licensing model," Education Week, 6.

Rodman, B. (September 9, 1987) "Two unions gain sharp pay hikes, role in decisions," Education Week, 7, 1, 25.

Rosenfeld, M., Thornton, R. F., & Skurnik, L. S. (1986) Analysis of the professional functions of teachers. Research Report 86-88, Princeton, New Jersey: Educational Testing Service.

Rosenshine, B., & Furst, N. F. (1971) "Researcher on teacher performance criteria" in B. O. Smith (Ed.) Research in teacher education: A symposium. Englewood Cliffs, N. J.: Prentice-Hall.

Rudner, L. M. (1987) What's happening in teacher testing. Washington, D. C.: U. S. Government Printing Office.

Schon, D. A. (1983) The reflective practitioner. New York: Basic Books, Inc., Publishers.

Shanker, A. (1985,a) "Separating wheat from chaff," Phi Delta Kappan, 67, 108-109.

Shanker, A. (1985,b) "A national teacher examination," Educational Measurement: Issues and Practices, 4, 28-31.

Shanker, A. (October 10, 1985) "Shanker urges a major restructuring of nation's schools," Teacher Education Reports, 7, 104.

Shulman, L. S. (1985) "The study of knowledge in teaching." American Educational Research Association, Chicago, Illinois.

Shulman, L. S. (1986) "Those who understand: Knowledge growth in teaching," Educational Researcher, 15, 4-14.

Shulman, L. S. (1987) "Assessment for teaching: An initiative for the profession," Phi Delta Kappan, 69, 38-44.

Smith, B. O. and Peterson, D. (January 31, 1986) Common Concerns of Florida Performance Measurement System use in the master teacher program. Letter.

Smith, D. C., & Neale, D. C. (1987) "The construction of expertise in primary science: Beginnings." American Educational Research Association, Washington, D. C.

Stephens, J. M. (1967) The process of schooling. New York: Holt, Rinehart, and Winston, Inc.

Streifer, P. A. (1987) "Validated teacher competency lists: A comparative analysis resulting in a generic model." American Educational Research Association, Washington, D. C.

Tamir, P. (1987) "Subject matter and related pedagogical knowledge in teacher education." American Educational Research Association, Washington, D. C.

Wilson, A. J. (1986) "Historical issues of validity and validation: The National Teacher Examinations." American Educational Research Association, San Francisco, California.

CHAPTER FOUR

OPACITY AS A POLICY FOR EDUCATIONAL POLICY

by

Robert D. Heslep
University of Georgia

Beginning with Socrates and continuing into the present, philosophers have tended to argue in favor of clarity and against opacity. Indeed, students of philosophy sometimes have wondered if their masters have not been belaboring the obvious. Despite their long established general agreement about clarity and obscurity, however, philosophers apparently have failed to persuade all educational policy makers about the respective values of these qualities. Some makers of educational policy have pleaded the merits of opacity, at least in certain situations; and more than a little legislation has been passed with vague or obscure meanings of key terms. A major example of such legislated policy is Public Law 94-142, or "The Education for All Handicapped Children Act of 1975," which has encouraged the mainstreaming in the public schools of millions of mentally retarded and otherwise handicapped persons. While this law contains explicit definitions of at least twenty-two terms, it contains no definition, explicit or not, of the central term "education."

It seems appropriate, therefore, to belabor the seeming obvious yet again. I shall open with an examination of various arguments from the policy literature that favor opacity in some measure for educational policies. Subsequently, I shall argue that the concept of a policy entails that clarity is always, not just in special situations, desirable for any educational policy and that opacity is always, not merely in some situations, undesirable for any educational policy.

Two kinds of objections to clarity as a policy in making educational policies are likely to be raised. One kind is concerned with methodology while the other is concerned with strategy.

The methodological objection is inspired by Aristotle's dictum that an inquirer should seek clarity only insofar as the subject-matter being investigated is amenable to clarification. Abstract and constant subject-matters, such as those of mathematics, natural science, and other theoretical disciplines, may be made fully perspicuous or nearly so whereas concrete and variable subject-matters, such as those of prudence, morality, statesmanship, and other practical disciplines, may be made only more or less clear. The making of educational policy is a practical matter; it aims at courses of action to be followed in particular situations, which are concrete and differ in detail from one to another. Accordingly, any attempt to render educational policies pellucid is unrealistic; it seeks that which cannot be obtained. Moreover, the effort fosters indifference toward local variances in policy implementation and, thus, encourages conflict.

This argument's basic premise is quite acceptable but it does not support the argument's conclusion. Precision of meaning is frequently something beyond the pale of policy making. The absurdity of always trying to put precision in educational policies was reflected by the behavioral objectives project, which held that educational goals could be stated with precision if only they were stated in terms of behavior. The difficulty, it was soon discovered, was that the behavior ingredient to any goal has a wide range of specificity and an indefinite variety. The premise, however, does not rule out any effort to make educational policies more or less clear. All that it excludes in this regard is the attempt to make educational policies clearer than they can be. It would have been one thing for Congress to have included in Public Law 94-142 a definition of "education" that was a bit fuzzy around the edges, but it was quite a different thing for it not to include a definition of the term at all. Opacity is not the only alternative to precision. Moreover, the premise does not lead to the point about indifference toward local variances. It would do this only if clarity necessarily excluded discretion. While a clear policy might exclude discretion in its implementation, it need not. Actually, one can exercise discretion in implementing a policy only insofar as the policy is clear. Discretion entails knowledge and understanding of that with which one is dealing; hence, it entails that that with which one is dealing is perspicuous.

The kind of argument concerned with strategic matters has several variations. One of them maintains that an insistence upon clarity for each and every educational policy might disrupt the policy making process. This species was reflected by Henry Kissinger when he explained why clarity is not necessarily desirable in policy making: by always insisting upon clarity, policy makers might bog down in prolonged wrangles over definitions of terms and thus never adopt any policies. The educational terms that appear in educational policies often are ambiguous at best and sometimes are quite vague. Accordingly, the process of making educational policy is especially susceptible to unresolved disputes in efforts to clarify the terms of such policy; and the formulators and adopters of educational policy must be prepared to settle for some vagueness when the quest for clarity threatens the policy making process. If further clarification of an educational policy is necessary for implementing the latter, it can be had following the adoption process through procedures for conflict resolution, notably, an amendment process or the judicial process.

This argument contains two dubious presumptions. First, it presumes that there is something about the clarification of terms that causes disruption of the policy making process; second, it presumes that an enacted vague policy is better than no policy at all. As to the first presumption, it is acknowledged that policy making occasionally does bog down in contention over definitions; but it is insisted that this need not happen because there is something about the act of clarification that upsets policy making. It well might be that the policy makers use quarrels over definitions as screens behind which to hide other policy differences. Hence, even if policy makers accepted vague definitions, they still might disrupt the policy process by using something else as a contention of convenience. As to the second presumption, it has to be noted that if a vague policy is to be implemented it will have to be clarified in order to provide guidance for its implementation. But that it can or should be clarified by third parties during the implementation phase is questionable. For one thing, those who attempt to define terms during implementation might engage in hopeless dispute as readily as the original formulators of the policy did. For another thing, the third parties will not be able to divine what the initial policy formulators might have intended by the vague terms and thus might impose constrictions upon the terms that too might engender disruptions of the implementation process.

Another argument concerned with strategy maintains that clarity in educational policies might be socially disruptive. According to the argument no public policy is likely to benefit every member of the given society; indeed, the public policies of any society, it is sometimes held, regularly impose burdens upon certain groups within the society. To avoid social disturbances from a society's members that are likely to be adversely affected by a public policy, the formulators of the policy should render obscure the policy's negative importance for these members; and they can do this by leaving the meanings of at least some of the policy's terms vague. Hence, it perhaps was thought best to be silent in PL 94-142 on what education is so as to obscure the point that many handicapped students are to receive under the law much in the way of educational support services and something in the way of social adjustment but not much, perhaps very little, in the way of academic instruction.

An obvious fault with this argument is its unexamined cynical view of public policy, which is that any public policy is a measure ultimately for lining the pockets of one group by taking benefits from the pockets of another. An additional flaw is the argument's presumption that social disruption is necessarily bad. As in the case of the Civil Rights Movement, social disturbance might arise for good reasons. Finally, this argument frees policy makers from recognizing that a social disturbance engendered by a policy is a sign that something might be wrong with the policy.

The last objection related to the strategic use of opacity in educational policy rests on the point that definitions set limits. To define a meaning is to distinguish it from other meanings. Accordingly, to clarify a policy is to set limits on what it does and does not mean. In the eyes of at least some educational policy makers, the clarification of an educational policy might be disadvantageous as to the benefits that one might hope to gain through the policy; for such clarification means that one might exclude oneself from some benefits that otherwise might be gained through the policy. A concrete reflection of this position is found in a statement made by a witness before the Senate committee that drafted the Senate's version of the Education for All Handicapped Children Act of 1975. The witness, who was the Executive

Secretary of the Council of Administrators of Special Education, Inc., intimated that neither the term "education" nor the term "all children" should be defined for the reason that various interpretations of the terms "have deprived many children of their rights." Thus, rather than regarding vagueness as an obstacle to understanding and implementation, the supporters of an educational policy should recognize vagueness as an opportunity for obtaining benefits that others might think to be beyond that policy. The procedures for obtaining benefits in the face of policy vagueness is occasionally called "duking it out in court" and "getting all that you can steal."

That this argument involves difficulties should be apparent. For one thing, it is an invitation to clog the implementation stage of the public policy process by deliberately transferring the clarification function from the formulation to the implementation stage. For another, it is not evident why one should believe that more benefits will be obtainable at the implementation stage rather than the formulation one. Clarification must take place at some stage; and according to the argument, when there is clarification at the implementation or any other stage, there will be limits and thus losers and gainers. Only if there is reason to believe that one has more control over implementation than one has over formulation would one have ground for pursuing this tactic. Why one should believe this is not plain. Finally, this argument views public policy from the standpoint of prudence rather than from that of morality or social justice. Such policy is most appropriately deemed from one of the latter viewpoints. While the argument at hand speaks of rights and benefits, it intends not rights and benefits necessarily of the members of the public but those of some individual or the members of some group not necessarily identifiable with the public.

I now will argue why educational policies should be clear. Just as the term "policy" may be used to refer to both an outcome and the process leading to it, "educational policy" may be employed to mean both. But just as "a policy" normally signifies an outcome and never a process, "an educational policy" usually refers to a product and never a process. Accordingly, the analysis of what an educational policy is should focus upon an outcome even though it might seek some understanding of the product by looking at the process connected with it. Common discourse contains such expressions as "to state a policy," "policy statement," and "a statement of policy." It may be taken then, as treating a policy as a statement.

A statement is an utterance, which means that it essentially has an utterer and a context. The utterer may be an individual or a collective body, e.g., a government. But a statement is not an aimless utterance; it logically is addressed to some party or parties, who may be called its "recipient" or "recipients." A recipient of a statement may be the one and the same person as its utterer or a different person. A statement, of course, is not just any utterance with a recipient; it is propositional or normative. If the former, it is confirmable or disconfirmable; if the latter, it is justifiable or unjustifiable. Because an utterance without meaning can be neither confirmed nor disconfirmed nor justified nor unjustified, a statement must be a meaningful utterance. Even though a statement is made typically via one or more meaningful sentences, it may not be identified with a sentence or cluster of sentences or even with the sentence's or cluster's meaning. The reason is that the same sentence or sentence cluster may be used to make different statements, depending upon who the utterer and the recipient are and what the contexts are.

In that normal talk regards a policy as a statement, it agrees with the view that a policy is a communication or declaration of intent; but it certainly does not mean that a policy is just any kind of communication or declaration of intent. Being neither true nor false, policies are not propositions; being justifiable or unjustifiable, they are normative statements. The kind of normative statement a policy is, is a directive; a policy approvingly points to a goal to be pursued or to an action to be performed so as to attain the goal or to both. A policy's utterer might state only an action to be performed so as to attain the goal or to both. A policy's utterer might state only an action to be performed if he or she believes that the goal of the action is already evident and acceptable to the policy's recipients. On the other hand, the utterer might state only a goal if he or she simply wants to clarify or institute the end of some action already being performed.

That a policy is a statement does not imply that the policy can be fully understood by examining the statement simpliciter. Because a statement has a context in which it is uttered, it might be completely comprehensible only if it is related to its context. If nothing else, the context, possibly involving psychological, economic, political, and legal forces, might help explain why the policy was made and what its utterer intended it to mean. Also, because a policy statement is to be followed and well might have to be implemented, it might be totally understandable only if it is related to whatever compliance with there is and whatever implementation of it there is. Being concrete matters; compliance and implementation can reveal something of what policies mean for the concrete world. Thus, one way of grasping some of the concrete significance of the desegregation policy set forth in Brown vs. Topeka is to study compliance with and implementation of the policy.

That a policy is a statement of a directive has special bearing on the importance of clarity for educational policies. As already indicated, a statement is conveyed through some linguistic structure, which is commonly one or more sentences. Some linguistic structures, e.g., those of mathematics, the natural sciences, and engineering, are quite unambiguous and clear in meaning whereas others are more or less ambiguous and vague. Terms and sentences used in discourse about education tend to be ambiguous and vague. The ambiguity of the term "education" is widely recognized. Examples of other vague educational terms are "teaching," "learning," and "curriculum." When sentences contain ambiguous and vague educational terms, they too are ambiguous and vague. Thus, the sentence, "Teaching includes learning," is ambiguous because there is a sense of the former terms, which is ambiguous as well as vague, in which teaching logically includes the attainment of learning and a sense in which it does not. In the sense of getting someone to learn something, teaching necessarily includes the attainment of learning and a sense in which it does not. In the sense of getting someone to learn something, teaching necessarily includes learning as an attainment, but in the sense of trying to get someone to learn something, teaching does not necessarily include learning as an attainment.

The terms and sentences used to express educational policies frequently include those characteristic of educational discourse. Thus, teacher merit pay policies, which usually prescribe that pay to teachers be distributed according to their efforts in bringing about learning, generally utilize the terms "instruction," "teaching," "student," and "learning." Because the language through which educational policies are expressed is somewhat ambiguous and vague, it tends to render such policies unsettled in meaning and thereby, susceptible to disputes over what they mean. With respect to Public Law 94-142, for instance, the absence of an articulate conception of education has left a semantic vacuum that has been filled by the preconceived and diverse notions of education held by parents, school boards, judges, and others. As one commentator has noted, the vagueness of Congress' intention and the ambiguity of the term "education" have led interested parties "to develop expectations and assumptions about what the state must provide to a handicapped child by way of education" and thus to engage in litigation when their expectations and assumptions have not been realized. So, because educational policies logically can direct action only to the extent that they are clear in meaning, they logically need to be clear in meaning.

By way of conclusion a proleptical objection will be met. Some people might think that my argument advocating clarity for educational policies has a simplistic view of policy conflicts. More specifically, they might think that the argument allows conflict avoidance but excludes conflict resolution and thus suggests that there need be no conflicts related to the meanings of policies after those meanings are clarified. After all, the argument's insistence upon clarity aims at the avoidance of conflicts and ignores conflict resolution altogether. It is agreed that the argument does ignore conflicts that might arise after policy meanings are clarified, but it also is denied that the argument excludes the possibility of such conflicts and the need for conflict resolution. The argument ignores conflict resolution not because it holds that policies should not involve it but because it focuses on a problem of educational policies that relates to conflict avoidance but not to conflict resolution. While the argument implicitly maintains that the clarification of meanings during the formulation phase of policy making will help avoid conflicts during the adoption and implementation application of policies, it does not deny that the application of policies, no matter how well they are clarified, requires an interpretation of particulars with respect to the meanings of the policies and thus that policies should incorporate some mechanism for settling disputes over such an interpretation. In short, I believe that the clarification of policy meanings avoids otherwise needless disputes and that policies need a procedural clause for dealing with unavoidable conflicts over the relationship between policy meanings and their referents.

CHAPTER FOUR

COMPARATIVE PERSPECTIVES ON THE AMERICAN
DROPOUT PROBLEM

by

Richard Renner
University of Florida

In the last few years there has developed a fear in the United States that an increase in academic standards might lead to a massive dropout of marginal students. This fear is fueled, in part, by the belief that in many countries the achievement of average and below average students is superior to our own. Since I am not persuaded that acceptance of mediocrity in high schools is educationally superior to minimum wage employment, I became interested in what some other countries have been doing in relation to this kind of problem.

What is a dropout? Put simply, it is a student who has failed to complete the level of education commonly attained in his community. It can take many forms. At one extreme, a study of dropouts in the Indian state of Karnataka found that only 33% completed the first four years of elementary school. When one considers that two-thirds of the fathers were illiterate and eighty percent are below the poverty line, this may not be an inconsiderable achievement (Seetharamu, 1985, pp. 3, 27, 37). Indeed, only 8.4% of the children had actually failed before dropping out (Seetharamu, 1985, p. 64). In quite a different setting, in Canada's Northwest Territory, fewer than ten percent of the native pupils who start kindergarten ever finish 12th grade (Hall, 1986, p. 33). There are also those who have never even dropped in. In 1974, for example, 22% of Mexico City's population and 66% in southern Mexico had no schooling at all (Hernandez Medina, 1978, p. 35). In most sub-Saharan countries lack of schooling is even more common. In the USA, in New York, Boston and Chicago, nearly half of high school students do not finish (Rumberger, 1987, p. 117). It seems that dropout is a relative matter. In fact, Americans now in their eighties and nineties with only eight years of formal schooling were never thought of as dropouts; their eight-year elementary program was intended to be terminal. Finally, what is terminal? Consider the successful secondary students in Leningrad who did not go on to further study, even though their grades were quite adequate. Of course, 27% did not pass the competitive entrance examination to the higher education equivalent course; 62% expressed no desire for further study; 42% preferred financial independence; and 36% cited financial difficulties (Vasileva, 1976, p. 53). Indeed does increasing the required years of schooling, which increases school attendance, make the dropout problem more acute? Experts (Rumberger, 1987, p. 101, and Barber and McClellan, 1987, pp. 264-67) admit that the dropout concept is ill-defined and correspondingly difficult to analyze. Given these uncertainties, a look at the problem from the perspective of other countries may prove helpful.

To begin, Americans are less inclined to make the social class distinctions which continue to exist in Western Europe. American belief is that everyone ought to be equal, and if not, the public school should provide an opportunity to become so. The American student has a certain freedom to reject such an opportunity; however, those who do are regarded as irresponsible for having rejected a key value of the American secular faith. Therefore, our public educators vigorously discourage early school leaving, not just because they embrace core American values and the school's role in promoting them, but also to absolve themselves of responsibility for the student's apparent irresponsibility. Americans link early withdrawal to a failure of democracy and do not like to be reminded that there may be citizens in our midst to whom the school has little to offer.

In fact, American public schools have long been structured to discourage dropouts. Progressive educational ideology--I use the term ideology in the sense that is a belief system not to be criticized or challenged but only to be refined and improved--has enabled American public schools, which are based on norm-referenced amount-of-time-served criteria, to push wide-ranging and often undemanding electives along with individualized and learner-centered instruction, as important stratagems to integrate and retain the majority of the youth cohort in school. Such all-inclusive approaches have the effect of circumventing the establishment of firm standards which might induce the uncommitted, the uncertain, and the undecided to withdraw. In the same vein, the popular notion that almost any school-sponsored activity can contribute to significant pupil growth further serves to justify retention of pupils past a point of no return. This is not to argue that the features sketched above are without merit but that their ubiquity as the principal rationale for public schools practice makes the potential for dropout widespread.

Outside the USA, concern about dropouts, though growing is much less common. The term "school leaver" is usually preferred because it describes rather than deplores withdrawal. Indeed, tracking, long practiced in Western Europe, sorts out students with the result that one of the appropriate student options is early withdrawal, usually to enter the workplace. Widespread acceptance of social class differences also makes dropout less stigmatizing than in the USA.

At the same time, one of the principal devices used in many countries to assure that instructional efforts have been effective is the "public" or external (state or national) examinations which link the teacher's efforts more closely to an eventual systematic demonstration by the student that certain standards of knowledge or performance have been attained. Such devices offer opportunity to anyone of demonstrated talent, no matter how humble his origin, and serve as a sort of egalitarian corrective in societies noted for their social inequality. Such performance-oriented policies are, to a considerable extent, products of the highly professional national bureaucracies which emerged in 19th century continental Europe as a means of promoting national political and military self-preservation (Ramirez and Boli ,1987, pp. 2-17). A country's strength rested in the efficient development of all citizens able to profit from further schooling, no matter how modest their origins. However, unlike most American accountability examinations which are used to assure the public that a minimal level has been attained, the European examinations are concerned with measuring superior achievement. Indeed, they usually deny high status schooling to those unable to demonstrate superior competence.

This is not to suggest that the less successful European children are encouraged to drop out. Usually they are shunted into separate schools, or separate tracks within comprehensive schools which are commensurate with their achievement and, one suspects, where their presence no longer interferes with the quality of instruction provided to the more talented. Still, in France, Italy, Germany, and Sweden, only 12%, 18%, 10%, and 8% respectively did not complete compulsory schooling in a normal way (OECD, 1985, p. 63). However, here, as the age of compulsory education has been increased, so too has the difficulty of engaging the enthusiasm of prospective school leavers. One boy, employed in the United Kingdom as a clerk said, "I found that at school we were only taught to pass exams....We were not educated about life....I discovered in my school life that I went to, listened to, and learned more from teachers who had worked outside the education circle. Perhaps it was coincidence" (OECD, 1983, p. 50). In England, where public examinations at age 16 and 18 identify superior achievers, an additional mid-range Certificate of Secondary Examination (CSE) has been used to motivate many in the lower 70% who might not be able to achieve at a high standard. That such average scores have been taken seriously by employers in making hiring decisions testifies to the value of intermediate level measures of achievement. In America, granting employers easy access to students' standardized achievement test scores, with student permission, of course, might be a start. A somewhat related point is that nearly fifty percent of young Americans in 1985 who did not complete the 12th grade studied for the GED and 40 percent of those received it, thus securing a minimum job-entry credential. It should also be noted unlike the USA, the bureaucracies responsible for both schooling and employment placement are generally part of the same broad administrative structure. This facilitates the transition of marginal youth out of schooling and into employment.

What do perspective dropouts need most? Should they acquire attitudes and skills more closely linked to workplace expectations? A study of elementary pupils in the Philippines concluded that the way to develop favorable work attitudes was not by increasing the learning time for manual work but rather through the mind, that is, through subjects that have a high intellectual content (Hernandez Medina, 1978, p. 266). Another conclusion was that if effective workplace attitudes are to be developed, recourse should be made to a medium other than schools. In Japan, on the other hand, although 94 percent of compulsory school leavers transfer to the upper-secondary level, the low achievers, (about 30 percent of the cohort) are directed to vocational schools (OECD, 1985, p. 108).

As for vocational schools, in many countries they tend to be "pale copies" of general academic schools while their are teachers and facilities are usually more expensive to maintain. Even when well-supported they tend to be substandard considering what they attempt to do (Hernandez Medina, 1978, pp. 263-64). Because of its higher cost vocational education benefits ought to exceed those from other types of schooling. Usually this is not the case. In Columbia and Tanzania, diversified vocational secondary education did not prove to offer measurable monetary advantages to students over conventional schools (Psacharopoulos, 1985, p. 227) suggesting that it is a poor strategy for reducing premature school withdrawal. In Egypt, vocational schools tended to function as a roundabout way of gaining access to university with such students spending valuable time learning practical skills they are unlikely ever to use (Hernandez Medina, 1978, pp. 263-64).

On the other hand, Marxist polytechnical theory makes important claims in behalf of the moral and intellectual benefits of actual labor, no matter how menial that may be. Even in practice Soviet education gives considerable attention to labor activity in school or school-like contexts although the reality of the experience is often quite unauthentic. Japanese schools, on the other hand, have few dropouts, partly because the status rankings of the various secondary schools are quite clearly linked to the quality of job opportunities of those who persist. In addition, because effort is a celebrated cultural value, pupils are expected to "tough it out" and learn to tolerate the difficult. According to literary critic Suichi Kato, Japanese education "is designed to produce very good mediocre people" and Japan may have the best educated lower half of its population of any country in the world (Fallows, 1987, pp. 20-24). Its homogeneous group-oriented society also helps the teacher to impose a values consensus on her charges so that nearly all internalize a responsibility for diligence. Then too, the teacher usually advises her charges from a basis of authority while in the USA, the child's right, indeed need, for self-determination is so valued that teachers are often reluctant to impose their "middle class" values on marginal pupils. Indeed, it is awkward for them to admit that they are marginal. As a consequence, many of the characteristic psychological and cultural problems which handicap marginal youth are not openly acknowledged or frankly discussed in school.

A start at filling the vacuum is to recognize that marginals are a different social class. But if they are, then what? For Americans, their answer is empty. But consider the following slogan drawn from plaques that once adorned 19th century English laboring men's reading rooms and which echo their distrust of employers:

> Here we may utter with a freeman's tone,
> Sound truth's--for why? The building is our own. (Hopkins, 1985, p. 30)

Consider also whether the following statement by Henri de Man (Hopkins, 1985, p. 31) may be true enough but too radical for American schools. If it is, then the curricular vacuum which erstwhile "working class" dropouts confront has been demonstrated:

> When labor strikes, it says to its Master
> I shall no longer work at your command.
> When labor organizes a part of its own, it says
> I shall no longer vote at your command
> When labor creates its own schools, it says
> I shall no longer think at your command.

If, as American political rhetoric assumes, we are already free and equal, then public schools should serve all social sectors equally well, including those at the margin. However, since local boards are usually dominated by well-intending but conservative members of the upper middle class, it is unlikely that curricular knowledge of inspirational value to working-class pupils will enjoy a high priority, if any at all. It is even difficult for liberals who support the cause of the disadvantaged to imagine what such a curriculum ought to include, let alone the seeking out of teachers competent to teach it. However, subject matter such as lawful strategies for organizing rent boycotts, how to form voting blocs, how to organize and fund independent leadership groups, where to buy the best local bargains, how to organize a cooperative, how to set up a small business, the economic value of good work habits, successful labor heroes, etc., would encourage many of our poor to begin the climb out of poverty. Of course state-managed schools in other long-established democracies seldom teach such activist citizens skills either.

Another common reason for dropout in the USA is attendance at schools with high rates of disorder and indiscipline (McDill, 1986, p. 157). Disorder is less common in more authoritarian social systems; put differently, the USA is one of the most anti-authoritarian of the industrialized nations. It is not surprising then that our incidence of school disorder is greater. Pregnancy is also an important cause although nearly half of these are reported to result in abortions. However, in countries such as Austria, which, incidentally, is 84 percent Roman Catholic, easy availability of condoms from vending machines at community locations helps make this cause of dropout less likely.

A quarter of American male dropouts give as a reason for early withdrawal that they have been offered a job (McDill, 1986, p. 141; Borus, 1984, p. 2) in a general survey of over 6,000 American youths age 16-21 found that some 56% were employed. Of those providing hourly rate of pay information, nearly one-fourth were in jobs paying less than the minimum wage. Since over half said they would accept work at or below the minimum wage, it seems that there is a substantial desire to engage in productive effort of some kind.

Switzerland, Germany and Austria are prominent among fewer than a dozen countries which offer apprenticeship opportunities. These provide, usually at very low pay, a means for youth to master, over a period of years, a particular trade (OECD, 1985, pp. 46-47). The state and representatives of the skilled trades collaborate closely to provide extensive hands-on experience in dozens of skilled occupations. German schools require that in addition to on-the-job duties, such workers attend special classes one or two days per week until age 18 to assure that they develop not only as responsible citizens, but personally and culturally as well.

Some schools also recognize the potential school leaver's interest in getting a job by introducing courses about work, by defining and restructuring schooling as a form of work, or by simulating work in the curriculum (OECD, 1983, pp. 51-52). But the direct learning experiences so vital to prospective dropouts such as sticking to time schedules, observing contracts, relating personally to adults and fellow workers, drawing wages, putting in a full day, learning to tolerate tedium, etc., is extremely difficult to replicate in a school setting where humane as well as productivity considerations are expected. On the other hand, for those students planning to enter white collar professions, dropout is seldom considered because for them the academic life is more directly vocational and corresponds closely to the job situations they will encounter in adult life.

Although school programs which sponsor actual work experience would seem to be more effective than merely studying about jobs, a German survey of such participants showed that their rates of representation among the youthful employed and unemployed was about the same as for non-program participants (OECD, 1983, p. 76). Similar results have been reported for Scottish school leavers. The OECD observes that independently organized part-time work seems to facilitate further employment somewhat more than special work experience programs (OECD, 1983, p. 76).

Not entering the job market may be productive. The survey of primary school dropouts' parents in Karnataka, India found that 23% were needed to do household chores; 18.2% to care for younger children; 14.6% to rear cattle. Only 15.1% they said, left school for lack of interest. A majority of school-leavers worked from five to eight hours a day. One in five was engaged in paid labor (Seetharamu, 1985, pp. 50, 68). One wonders about the contribution American dropouts may be making when they free up others for gainful employment. Interestingly, a review of an American Enterprise Institute study claims that U.S. Bureau of Labor Statistics data from a 1984 survey reveal that in the USA, in the poorest 20 percent of households, total expenditures are more than three times their reported pre-tax incomes (Novak, 1987, pp. 42-43).

For a poor family, the opportunity cost of a youth's schooling can be very high, even if tuition itself is free. This is especially true if all of a family's working hands are needed for a decent life. Subsidies to the student help to reduce this burden. Germany provides grants at the elite upper secondary level which serve to reduce student costs by about one-third; England has given substantial stipends to upper secondary and university students who show promise and demonstrate need; Australia has given cash allowances to high school students planning to enter teaching; France has provided modest "clothing" allowances to all school children so that none can claim social disadvantages in dress in order to excuse absence from school. Until recently, the USA has rarely used attendance inducements. It has long provided free lunches to impecunious pupils; however, that program was conceived more with the disposal of subsidized farm surpluses in mind than discouraging dropout. However, beginning in 1988, Wisconsin became the first state to tie the school attendance of 13 to 19 year olds to benefits paid under Aid to Families with Dependent Children. This "Learnfare" program also includes teenage parents (Mallozzi, 1988, pp. 7-8). Currently, in Massachusetts, youthful labor is said to be in such short supply due to abundant military contracts that some manufacturers are giving high school scholarships to talented poor children in the hope that they will work for them when they graduate.

A different alternative is to readily allow school-leaving with the proviso that the student may resume his schooling when he is more mature or more convinced of its value. One Swedish teenager agreed that students should go to school first and then try working; then they should be allowed to return to school or leave as they wish. "I think this is a good thing," he observed, "because then you know what it is your are letting yourself in for. I found out what it is like having a job. I was never told about it in school." (OECD, 1983, pp. 24-25)

The underlying policy problem is that school leavers lacking any prospect of jobs can become social problems. Yet for the school to retain them means that teaching comes to be driven by warehousing rather than educational considerations. Unions, as potent forces in democratic industrial nations, are well aware that unneeded young workers may depress wages; they are also more comfortable with the notion that added years of compulsory schooling imply greater opportunity for workers' children and thus they tend to accept schooling even when it is custodial. In any case, Denmark is one country which makes it easier for dropout reentry with its long-established tradition of "after-schools." It is possible to receive governmental funding to cover up to 85% of the expenses of a private residential school; all that is required is a 'supporting group' of at least fifty people who can testify to the need, a curriculum framework that satisfies fundamental education criteria and a headmaster and teachers whose credentials the state will accept (White, 1980, pp. 5, 18). Denmark has 120 such after-schools which enroll a substantial proportion of working class youth.

The western European nations' general regard for firm standards and respect for authority makes them more willing to justify early school-leaving than the USA which is inclined to regard schooling as accessing opportunity and self-discovery. Yet a serious negative aspect of the schooling which many average-ability European majorities receive is the tendency of their teachers to communicate low expectations to their charges. An English boy employed as a Venetian blind fitter said, "After my second year at school my class was just thrown aside as we did not qualify for "O" levels. So, he said, it was a case of 'to hell with you'." Or, "We would go into school in the morning and get sent home two hours later. Out of all the last year-and-a-half you could have put what we were taught into three months." For him, leaving such schooling made good sense. An English girl observed that, "Most of our teachers concentrated on bright pupils--encouraging them--which is wrong because bright people get on fine without help, while the less able are moved into a lower non-certificate class...." Another dropout perceived the teachers' attitude to be, "We have to put up with them until they reach SLA (school leaving age), we'll have to keep them occupied until then, with no care about preparing them for life outside school in any way." (OECD, 1983, p. 25). One study found that there is a substantial group of students in American high schools similar in background to those who dropout but who stay on to graduation. Yet the latter group reports less growth in self esteem than either the dropout or the college bound (Wehlage, 1986, pp. 386-87). Psychologically, such warehousing may be worse than laboring at low pay.

The alienation which fosters dropout may also be enhanced by the rigidity and formalization of the educational process which is a product of the development of large secondary schools, especially in the USA, Japan, Scandinavia, but also in urban areas elsewhere. When the informal face-to-face social control that can be exercised in the small school breaks down, then all kinds of formal restrictions, which require an elaborate system of rules backed up by increasing administrative machinery, have to be substituted. The result is an ethos of unstable relationships between students and school staff.

Truancy, vandalism and harassment can thrive when students violate formal regulations without having to suffer the personal embarrassment and shame which is inevitable in a small setting (OECD, 1985, pp. 86-87).

As already noted, dropout is more serious when there are few jobs. The implied promise in the post war period of benefits to all from access to abundant educational opportunity seems to have lost its luster. Economic recession further diminishes the value of the educational credential and fosters doubts about the once fashionable notion of more and more schooling. Raising the years of compulsory schooling without asking how much is enough is often disastrous.

The situation may be less acute in countries with broad-based national youth service programs. Such programs are not necessarily narrowly military nor even compulsory; many assign tasks to youth which shore up weak points in the civilian infrastructure. In Tanzania, national service has been paramilitary and emphasized civic work in villages and police duties; it also sought to inculcate socialist attitudes and served many as a stepping stone to government service (Leonor, 1985, p. 260). The USA Peace Corps has played a similar role in advancing the domestic careers of many of its participants. The apparent need for civic experience in the USA as an alternative to so much schooling is suggested by a 1979 survey which asked American teenagers what they owed their country. From the majority the reply was "Nothing." (Noah, 1986, pp. 35-41).

This essay has drawn on a variety of foreign settings in an effort to show how they can enlarge our awareness of the meaning of dropout in the USA. However, whatever remedies have been mentioned contribute more to an understanding of the issues rather than advocacy of a particular solution. Nonetheless, it would be remiss not to endorse one unusually well-conceived effort. An experimental program reported by Hall, (1986, pp. 33-38) stands out in its appeal to the employment interests of dropout-prone students while it continues to retain them more years in school.

As previously noted, in Canada's Northwest Territory fewer than 10 percent of the native pupils who start kindergarten actually finish grade 12. Until 1983, all programs in the Northwest Territory led to grade 12 graduation. An experimental project known as the Community Occupation Program designed specifically for students about to drop out, was created by the Department of Education and has since expanded from two to eight schools. Students must be 15 or older, unlikely to reach a grade ten school standard, and interested in being in the program. No one is admitted until his parents are counseled about reasons for the placement and sign a consent form. At 15, students are too young for admission to adult education programs. In 1983, the first Community Occupational Program was pilot tested in a Dogrib Indian community about 100 kilometers from Yellowknife. The 16 students who began in the program had a history of poor attendance, low achievement scores, and because of parental ethnic background, little family support and guidance. In addition, the students' home language was different from that of most of their teachers. Before entering the program average attendance was 30%; two years latter 12 of the potential dropouts graduated with a successful attendance rate of 81%.

In the program itself, students spend mornings in class studying functional English and mathematics, personal development, career and life management, and options such as physical education and computers. The subject matter offered is intended to have immediate or near-future application and includes the filling out of forms, using the telephone, becoming careful consumers, and using leisure wisely. A single instructor is responsible for all aspects of the 15-student program including meeting with parents, locating suitable work stations, monitoring work experience and teaching the classes. The Department of Education assists in identifying useful teaching materials.

The experiential portion of the program requires that at least 15 different employers be found who are willing to take part. This itself is often quite a feat in communities which have almost no economic base. With employer advice, skill profiles are drafted for each work station in the community. The cleaning/ laundry work station, for example, specifies 18 different tasks. Students generally spend afternoons or evenings working at these locations and change over to a different one every 2 to 6 weeks. Employers are asked to evaluate each student on employee traits such as punctuality and ability to follow directions. In this manner, students learn to make responsible decisions and acquire experience which leads to a sense of accomplishment.

No program can be taken seriously unless it has clear standards. For the Community Occupational Program the graduation requirements are:
1. 80% attendance and punctuality. One youth who missed the school but was so dedicated to the program that he traveled 15 kilometers by dog team in order not to miss class.
2. Three good-to-excellent work experience evaluations from employers worked with for at least one month.
3. Completion of a job preparation project with real or mock interviews, the writing of a personal resume, and the preparation of a profile of a job in the community the student would like to have.
4. The performance of community service work.
5. Completion of the standardized test of Adult Basic Education with a follow-up counseling session.

A certificate, signed by the Minister of Education, is awarded after these requirements have been met.

The overall thesis has been that as young adults, many dropouts find little of value in the schools. Sometimes this is the result of serious gaps in the formal curriculum, sometimes it is a result of poorly conceived and badly managed schools, sometimes it may be due to the fact that what schools attempt to do for or to those young adults may be socially and psychologically inappropriate. It concludes that early withdrawal, easy return to further education, facilitation of gainful employment and greater opportunity for participation in public service may be constructive practices. It suggests that some dropouts are alienated by the immaturity and/or mediocrity of what their schools offer them in their particular, often disadvantaged socioeconomic circumstances. It implies that dropout may carry a heavier stigma in America than elsewhere although at the same time our schools may be more likely to encourage valuable attitudes of optimism than is the case in many industrial countries. It acknowledges that although reasons for dropout are many and disparate, this study's particular emphasis is about those students presumed to possess worthy reasons for rejecting further schooling. For them, withdrawal need not be a negative experience, especially since large numbers of youth are retained in school for reasons that have little to do with education. Finally, it should be emphasized that if government is to provide costly subsidies to educate some of its youth cohort, it should also be willing to provide a wider range of socially constructive opportunities of those who do not find further schooling to be valuable.

BIBLIOGRAPHY

Barber, Larry and Mary McClellan, "Looking at America's Dropouts: Who Are They? Phi Delta Kappan, 69: (4) 264-267.

Borus, Michael, (Ed.) (1984) Youth and the labor market. Kalamazoo: Upjohn Institute for Employment Research.

Fallows, James. (1987) "Gradgrind's heirs," The Atlantic, March, 259: 16=24.

Hahn, Andres. (1987) "Reaching out to America's dropouts: What to do?" Phi Delta Kappan, December, 69: (4), 256-263.

Hall, Barbara. (1986) "Alternate co-op education in Canada's North," Guidance and Counseling, March, 1: (4), 33-38.

Hernandez Medina, Alberto and Manzoor Ahmad. Education and youth in less-developed countries, Berkeley: Carnegie Foundation for the Advancement of Teaching.

Hopkins, Philip. (1985) Worker's education: An international perspective. Milton Keynes: The Open University Press.

Leonor, M. D. (Ed.) Unemployment, schooling and training in developing countries: Tanzania, Egypt, The Philippines and Indonesia. London: Croom Helm.

Mallazzi, Vincent M. (1988) "Tying welfare to school attendance," New York Times, January 3, Section 12, 7-8.

McDill, Edward, Gary Natriello and Aaron Pallas, (1986), "A population at risk: Potential consequences of tougher school standards for dropouts," American Journal of Education, February 9: (2), 135-181.

CHAPTER FOUR

IN THE EYE OF THE STORM: PUBLIC EDUCATION'S STRUGGLE WITH ALLEGED SECULAR HUMANISM IN MOBILE, ALABAMA - A VALUES APPROACH

by

Samuel M. Vinocur
University of South Alabama

Introduction

The intent of this paper is to note the value profiles of approximately 3,700 present and future teachers across a seventeen-year period at the University of South Alabama and to observe and explore the nature and potential consequences of these values as they relate to the Religious Right's concerns and orientations. Based upon the results of the values of present and future teachers in Mobile, it is understandable why the Religious Right's "causes" receive a warm reception among many Southern educators.

Since the early 1980s Alabama has been a leading area of judicial controversies regarding church-state entanglements. The last judicial blockbuster occurred March 4, 1986, when a local federal judge, W. Brevard Hand, ruled "secular humanism" is a religion under the provisions of the First Amendment. Public schools, he declared, are illegally promoting it and discriminating against "theistic" religions. Major players in, and supporters of, Judge Hand's decision were various groups of the "Religious Right." Most notable among them were members of the tele-evangelist and Presidential candidate Pat Robertson's organization. Judge Hand's adoption of the term "Secular Humanism" is the first instance of a federal judge looking favorably on one of the Religious Right's favorite campaign tools.

Supporting Judge Hand's decision were 624 litigants residing in the Mobile area, many of whom were teachers and parents of students in the local public school system

The Religious Right has been active during the 1980s at trying to lower or eliminate the "wall of separation" between church and state in the nation's public elementary and secondary schools.

The city of Mobile, Alabama, has been a focal point form many of the Religious Right's concerns. Two recent major court cases of national consequence evolved out of litigation centered in Mobile, Alabama: Wallace vs Jaffree - regarding the promotion of prescribed prayers in public schools and Smith v Board of School Commissioners - regarding the banning of books and the promotion of "secular humanism."

Some of the educational and social orientations associated with the Religious Right have been noted by Ben Brodinsky who observes the following goals promoted by the New and Religious Right: Promoting prayer in public schools; promoting creationism; censoring textbooks and school library books; ending unionism and union tactics in education; promoting the interests of Christian schools; nurturing conservative ideas; fighting "secular humanism" in public schools; anti-busing for desegregation purposes; the fostering of anti-scientific beliefs; and the promotion of supernaturalism, mysticism and miraculism.[1] Secular humanism has become for these groups "...an all purpose, all inclusive charge that covers sins, both real and imaginary, actions committed or not committed."[2] Secular Humanism has become for the Religious Right a "catch all" concept for those "evils" noted, e.g., secular scientific rationalistic, and pluralistic views of life.

The Importance of Values for Educators

Because values are so central to human behavior, the task of all those concerned with the improvement of education is to better understand the values of all major groups that affect the school. The avoidance of problems rests in great measure upon the roles values play toward the motivation of individuals. Andrew Sikula notes the growing research literature that deals with the importance of values and value systems in such areas as "...personal goals, interpersonal conflict, group and cultural differences, human adaptability to change, organizational performance, occupation and career choice, and the like."[3]

Any value conflict between educators may negatively affect the roles of all groups in education. As Brian Sharples observes, "What is of value to people must be decided before the matters of process... and the degree to which values play a significant part depends on whether an issue is prone to value conflicts or more amenable to some intellectual analysis of the problem."[4]

The teacher's religious and ethnocentric values may cause classroom and administrative problems. Teacher bias has been known to affect negatively the learner as well as people in the community. The role of teachers as key agents in the socialization process makes their judgements and actions crucial to proper student behavior and educational outcomes.[5] Values serve as monitors of the limits of one's perceptions of ethical behavior[6] and they are basic elements in creation and development of personal goals, interpersonal conflict, group and cultural differences, and adaptability to change. They determine personal views of the world.[7]

Methodology

The nature of the population of our survey consists of approximately 3,200 future teachers (undergraduate students in education) and 500 teachers (graduate students in education) at the University of South Alabama. The percentage of females in this population is high, approximately eighty-five percent female in the undergraduate area and eighty percent in the graduate area.

The respondents to the survey were accorded complete anonymity in order to insure honesty of responses. Therefore, no attempt was made to gather information pertinent to age, gender, race, and the like.

The determination of the values of present and future educators in this paper emanates from the Rokeach Value Survey. Research indicates that values are not isolated units but clusters of related groups associated with comprehensive attitudinal and ideological dimensions. The social psychologist Milton Rokeach has developed a ranking self report which discerns two basic types of values each containing eighteen individual values. One set is called "terminal" values and represents certain end-states of existence or goals (for example, wisdom, salvation, a comfortable life). The other set is labeled "instrumental" values, such as honesty, courage, and broadmindedness, and represents means of achieving the ends or terminal values. Respondents are asked to rank-order the two sets of values. Additional description and explanation of the Rokeach Value Survey are beyond the scope of this paper but such information is readily available elsewhere.[8]

Each year of the seventeen-year period 1972-1988, the values of undergraduate students surveyed were aggregated to derive a yearly average. The same procedure was performed for graduate students (teachers) during a six-year time period, 1983-1988. Each of the eighteen "terminal" values was ranked on a basis of one through eighteen; the same procedure was used for the "instrumental" values. The ranking was plotted for each variable for each of the seventeen years. Non-parametric correlations were computed for the ranks among years. The significance of the study stems in part in the amazing consistency among the yearly ranking of values, as well as the specific constellation of values. Evidence of this is deduced via the utilization of Spearman's rho* and Kendall's W. (* available upon request).

The approach used in this study to determine the importance of present and future teacher profiles was performed by equally dividing the eighteen ranked terminal and eighteen instrumental values into two sectors, top and bottom. The midway rank--ninth--serves as a demarcation line separating the "higher" from the "lower" ranked values.

Findings and Interpretation

The findings from the study are summarized in the tables provided. The rankings of present and future teachers indicate that for the terminal and instrumental values both groups have a similar hierarchy of values. There are clear and discernible patterns of values for both the highest and lowest ranked values. In order to interpret the findings of the study, I use Rokeach's seven bipolar value categories that include within them clusters of values denoting orientations towards behavior.[9]

The value profiles of present and future teachers characterize these two groups as highly individualistic and religious people who strongly affirm familial orientations and positively value delayed gratification. Conversely, present and future teachers value far less societal concerns. They also have lower regard for values associated with competency (i.e., logical and imaginative) and intellectual orientations receive relatively low valuation.

Comparing the value orientations of present and future teachers, it is apparent the values of these groups (e.g., low rankings of equality, imaginative, and somewhat broadminded) conflict with openmindedness, inquiring, democratic beliefs, and tolerance associated with multicultural education.

Rokeach observes that individuals display highly dogmatic traits when they care less for equality, freedom, and being broadminded. They are more concerned with salvation.[10]

Feather also notes strong ethnocentric orientations associated with low rankings of equality and world of beauty.[11] The value profiles of present and future teachers correspond to Rokeach's and Feather's observations.

Regarding values and religious orientations Rokeach's studies reveal:

> All religious groups are similar in considering the values a world at peace, family, security, and freedom, the most important terminal values, and an exciting life, pleasure, social recognition, and a world of beauty the least important. Moreover, the religious, less religious, and nonreligious all agree in ranking the instrumental values honest, ambitious, and responsible highest, and imaginative, intellectual, logical, and obedient, lowest in importance....Two values--salvation and forgiving--stand out above all the others as the most distinctively Christian values.[12]

This study clearly shows that, with the exception of the values of a world at peace and ambitious, the value profiles of present and future teachers correspond to Rokeach's observations.

There is abundant scholarly literature nothing the close relationship between religion and prejudice. [13] Stark and Glock, noted authorities on religion and prejudice, make the controversial observation:

> Christian laymen, as a group, are a rather prejudiced lot. It is perfectly obvious that large numbers of people in the churches, for whom Christian ethics provide an important basis for love, understanding, and compassion, are not prejudiced. But the majority of church members are prejudiced; furthermore, they deny the right of the churches to challenge their prejudices.[14]

In reference to intolerance, Rokeach observes that individuals who are less racially and ethnically prejudiced rank <u>equality</u> higher than do those who are more tolerant of others.[15] He also notes, "...<u>equality</u>, is the value most predictive of behavior involving interracial relations."[16] The value of <u>imaginative</u> is closely associated with intolerance; low rankings of <u>imaginative</u> are generally associated with intolerant beliefs about others.[17]

In our study the low ranking of the value <u>equality</u> for present and future teachers combined with the low ranking of <u>imaginative</u> lends credence to the notion that present and future teachers may act intolerantly towards others.

Conclusion and Implications

The results of this study indicate the value profiles of present and future teachers are remarkably similar. These groups, via their ranking of values, are characterized as highly religious and individualistic. They possess strong familial orientations and affirm delayed gratification. However, present and future teachers rank far lower the values associated with social matters and concerns that are particularly affiliated with religious tolerance, multicultural orientations, and democratic inter-personal relations.

The values of present and future teachers in this study indicate that educators charged with developing and following school policies in our multicultural and democratic society may encounter value conflicts between the courts, themselves, and various members of a pluralistic community. Some results of this conflict could be the biased, ineffectual and unprofessional behavior of teachers as well as the subversion of scientific and democratically oriented curriculum and instruction.

Possibly complicating and frustrating attempts by school officials to enforce the laws and court decisions regarding church-state separation are the strong religious orientations of present and future teachers. There is likelihood that teachers who strongly possess religious value orientations will not challenge attempts by various religious organizations to introduce sectarian matters into the public schools. In fact, these teachers could favor religious indoctrination, school prayer, or even sectarian religiously oriented curricular matters.

One can expect teachers with strong religious and ethnocentric convictions, who also have a low valuation of being courageous, to favor or submit to the attempts of major sectarian power groups who desire to eliminate many multicultural and scientific concepts from the public schools.

Assuming the values of nearly four thousand students over a seventeen-year period are indicative of a substantial number of Mobilians in general, it is not surprising that the Religious Right and their concept of "secular humanism" has gained a strong hold in this community. As long as the value orientations noted in this paper continue in great measure, the assault upon public secular education will continue.

FOOTNOTES

1. Ben Brodinsky, "The New Right: The Movement and its Impact," *Phi Delta Kappan*, 64: 1982, 87-93.

2. Ibid., p. 90.

3. Andrew F. Sikula, "The Values and Value Systems of Governmental Executives," *Public Personnel Management*, vol. 2, Jan., 1973, p. 17.

See also Andrew F. Sikula, "Values and Value Systems: Importance and Relationship to Managerial and Organizational Behavior," Journal of Psychology, 78: 277-86.

4. Brian Sharples, "Values: The Forgotten Dimension in Educational Administration," Education Canada, vol. 24, 1984, pp. 32-37; also see condensed version, The Education Digest, vol. 50, April 1985, p. 19.

5. Thomas L. Good; Bruce J. Biddle; and Jere E. Brophy, Teachers Make a Difference (New York: Holt, Rinehart and Winston, 1975).

Jere E. Brophy and Thomas L. Good, Teacher-Student Relationships: Causes and Consequences (New York: Holt, Rinehart and Winston, 1974).

Frank H. Klassen and Donna M. Gollnick (Eds.) Pluralism and the American Teacher: Issues and Case Studies (Washington, D.C.: AACTE, 1977).

6. G. W. England, "Personal Value Systems of American Managers," Academy of Management Journal, March, 1967, pp. 53-68.

7. A. F. Sikula and J. P. Sikula, "The Values and Value Systems of Educational Administrators," paper presented at American Educational Research Association, annual meeting (57th, Chicago, IL, April, 1972) p. 2.

8. Milton Rokeach (Ed.) Understanding Human Values: Individual and Societal (New York: The Free Press, 1979).

Norman T. Feather, Values in Education and Society (New York: The Free Press, 1975).

9. Milton Rokeach, The Nature of Human Values (New York: The Free Press, 1973).

Norman T. Feather, op. cit.

10. Milton Rokeach, The Nature of Human Values, op. cit., pp. 114-116.

11. Norman T. Feather, op. cit., p. 141.

12. Milton Rokeach, The Nature of Human Values, op. cit., pp. 82-83.

13. Charles Y. Glock (Ed.) Religion in Sociological Perspective: Essays in the Empirical Study of Religion (Belmont, CA: Wadsworth Publishing Co., 1973).

Rodney Start and Charles Y. Glock, "Prejudice and the Churches," in Charles Y. Glock (Ed.), Religion in Sociological Perspective, op. cit.

14. Rodney Stark and Charles Y. Glock, "Prejudice and the Churches," op. cit., p. 91.

15. Ibid., p. 102.

16. Ibid., p. 159.

17. Norman T. Feather, op. cit., p. 140.

UNDERGRADUATE STUDENTS' YEARLY RANKING OF TERMINAL VALUES
1972-88

	1972	1973	1974	1975	1976	1977	1978	1979	1980	1981	1982	1983	1984	1985	1986	1987	1988	MEAN	MEDIAN
FREEDOM	1	1.0	5	5.0	3.5	3.0	5.0	6.0	6.5	6	6.0	8.0	6.0	4.0	5.0	8.0	9.0	5.17	5.00
MATURE LOVE	2	9.5	3	9.5	10.0	1.0	10.0	10.0	10.0	10	8.5	12.0	9.5	9.0	9.0	10.5	10.0	8.97	10.00
SALVATION	3	3.5	1	7.0	3.5	5.5	3.5	3.0	3.0	2	2.5	2.0	3.5	4.0	3.0	1.0	6.0	3.35	3.00
WORLD AT PEACE	4	6.0	10	9.5	11.5	12.0	11.0	11.5	9.0	11	11.0	10.5	11.0	11.0	11.0	13.0	12.0	10.29	11.00
SELF-RESPECT	5	5.0	2	2.0	1.0	1.0	1.0	1.0	1.0	1	1.0	1.0	1.0	2.0	1.5	3.0	1.0	1.79	1.00
WISDOM	6	2.0	6	3.0	6.0	5.5	6.0	5.0	8.0	5	7.0	7.0	7.5	7.0	8.0	7.0	7.0	6.05	6.00
FAMILY SECURITY	7	8.0	8	6.0	7.0	4.0	3.5	8.0	3.0	4	2.5	4.0	3.5	1.0	1.5	4.0	2.0	4.52	4.00
HAPPINESS	8	7.0	7	4.0	5.0	2.0	2.0	4.0	3.0	3	5.0	3.0	2.0	6.0	4.0	2.0	3.0	4.11	4.00
EQUALITY	9	11.0	11	12.0	11.5	11.0	12.0	11.5	12.0	12	12.0	10.5	12.0	12.0	13.0	14.0	13.0	11.73	12.00
INNERY HARMONY	10	3.5	4	1.0	2.0	7.0	8.0	2.0	5.0	7	4.0	5.0	5.0	4.0	6.0	6.0	4.0	4.91	5.00
TRUE FRIEND	11	9.5	9	8.0	8.0	8.0	7.0	7.0	6.5	8	10.0	6.0	7.5	10.0	7.0	5.0	5.0	7.79	8.00
SENSE OF ACCOM	12	12.0	12	11.0	9.0	9.0	9.0	9.0	11.0	9	8.5	9.0	9.5	8.0	10.0	9.0	8.0	9.70	9.00
NAT. SECURITY	13	14.0	15	15.0	14.0	16.0	14.0	16.0	13.5	15	14.0	13.0	15.5	14.0	14.0	16.0	15.0	14.52	14.00
COMFORT LIFE	14	13.0	13	13.0	13.0	13.0	13.0	13.0	13.5	13	13.0	14.0	13.0	13.0	12.0	12.0	11.0	12.91	13.00
WORLD BEAUTY	15	16.0	14	14.0	17.0	18.0	17.0	17.0	17.5	17	17.0	17.0	17.0	17.0	17.0	18.0	17.0	16.61	17.00
EXCITING LIFE	16	15.0	16	17.5	15.0	14.0	15.5	14.0	15.0	14	16.0	16.0	15.5	15.5	16.0	17.0	16.0	15.52	15.50
PLEASURE	17	18.0	17	16.0	16.0	15.0	15.5	15.0	16.0	16	15.0	15.0	14.0	15.5	15.0	15.0	14.0	15.58	15.50
SOC. RECOG	18	17.0	18	17.5	18.0	17.0	18.0	18.0	17.5	18	18.0	18.0	18.0	18.0	18.0	10.5	18.0	17.38	18.00

Kendall's W .898   Chi-Square 259.63 p < .0001

Table 2

UNDERGRADUATE STUDENTS' YEARLY RANKING OF INSTRUMENTAL VALUES
1972-88

	1972	1973	1974	1975	1976	1977	1978	1979	1980	1981	1982	1983	1984	1985	1986	1987	1988	MEAN	MEDIAN
HONEST	1	1.0	1.0	1.0	1.0	1.0	1.0	1.0	1.0	1.0	1	1.0	1.0	1.0	1.0	1.0	1.0	1.00	1.00
LOVING	3	4.0	3.0	3.0	2.5	3.0	3.0	3.0	2.5	3.0	3	2.0	2.5	3.0	3.0	2.0	3.0	2.85	3.00
HELPFUL	8	7.0	6.0	6.0	6.0	5.0	5.0	7.0	5.0	6.0	6	5.0	5.0	5.0	5.0	5.0	6.0	5.76	6.00
RESPONSIBLE	2	2.0	2.0	2.0	2.5	2.0	2.0	2.0	2.5	2.0	2	3.0	2.5	2.0	2.0	3.0	2.0	2.20	2.00
BROADMINDED	4	5.0	7.0	5.0	8.0	8.0	8.0	9.5	6.0	7.0	10	11.0	7.5	8.0	8.5	6.0	13.0	7.73	8.00
FORGIVING	9	3.0	4.0	4.0	4.0	4.0	4.0	4.0	4.0	4.0	4	4.0	4.0	4.0	4.0	4.0	4.0	4.23	4.00
INDEPENDENT	15	11.0	9.0	9.0	11.0	9.0	9.0	8.0	9.0	10.0	5	8.0	7.5	6.5	6.0	11.0	11.0	9.11	9.00
COURAGEOUS	7	10.0	12.0	12.5	14.0	14.0	15.0	15.0	11.0	12.0	12	13.0	13.0	15.0	14.0	14.0	15.0	12.85	13.00
CAPABLE	10	9.0	8.0	10.0	9.0	11.0	10.0	9.5	13.0	10.0	8	9.0	7.5	11.0	10.5	10.0	7.0	9.55	10.00
INTELLECTUAL	13	14.5	14.0	11.0	12.5	11.0	14.0	14.0	11.0	10.0	11	10.0	10.0	9.5	10.5	13.0	8.0	11.58	11.00
IMAGINATIVE	18	18.0	17.5	18.0	17.0	17.5	17.5	18.0	16.0	17.5	17	16.5	17.0	18.0	18.0	18.0	18.0	17.50	17.50
SELF-CONTROL	6	8.0	5.0	7.0	5.0	6.0	6.0	5.0	8.0	5.0	7	6.0	7.5	6.5	7.0	8.0	5.0	6.35	6.00
CHEERFUL	11	13.0	11.0	12.5	10.0	11.0	11.0	11.0	11.0	15.5	13	12.0	12.0	14.0	12.0	12.0	9.0	11.82	12.00
LOGICAL	16	14.5	16.0	16.0	16.0	16.0	16.0	16.0	17.0	14.0	14	16.5	16.0	16.0	16.0	16.0	14.0	15.64	16.00
POLITE	14	16.0	15.0	14.0	12.5	13.0	13.0	12.5	14.0	13.0	16	14.0	14.0	13.0	13.0	9.0	10.0	13.29	13.00
AMBITIOUS	5	6.0	10.0	8.0	7.0	7.0	7.0	6.0	7.0	8.0	9	7.0	11.0	9.5	8.5	7.0	12.0	7.94	7.00
OBEDIENT	17	17.0	17.5	17.0	18.0	17.5	17.5	17.0	18.0	17.5	18	18.0	18.0	17.0	17.0	17.0	17.0	17.41	17.50
CLEAN	12	12.0	13.0	15.0	15.0	15.0	12.0	12.5	15.0	15.5	15	15.0	15.0	12.0	15.0	15.0	16.0	14.11	15.00

Kendall's W .927   Chi-Square 267.88 p < .0001

Table 3

GRADUATE STUDENTS' YEARLY RANKING OF TERMINAL VALUES
1983-88

	1983	1984	1985	1986	1987	1988	MEAN	MEDIAN
FREEDOM	5.0	3.0	4.5	6.0	3.0	10.0	5.25	4.75
MATURE LOVE	9.0	9.0	8.0	10.0	10.0	7.0	8.83	9.00
SALVATION	7.5	4.5	2.0	5.0	5.0	3.0	4.50	4.75
A WORLD AT PEACE	10.0	10.0	10.0	11.0	14.0	12.0	11.16	10.50
SELF-RESPECT	1.0	1.0	1.0	1.5	8.0	2.0	2.41	1.25
WISDOM	6.0	6.0	9.0	8.0	7.0	4.0	6.66	6.50
FAMILY SECURITY	3.5	2.0	3.0	1.5	1.0	1.0	2.00	1.75
HAPPINESS	3.5	7.0	4.5	4.0	4.0	8.0	5.16	4.25
EQUALITY	13.0	12.5	14.0	13.0	18.0	14.0	14.08	13.50
INNER HARMONY	2.0	4.5	6.0	3.0	2.0	5.0	3.75	3.75
TRUE FRIENDSHIP	7.5	11.0	7.0	7.0	9.0	9.0	8.41	8.25
SENSE OF ACCOMPLISHMENT	11.0	8.0	11.0	9.0	6.0	6.0	8.50	8.50
NATIONAL SECURITY	15.0	12.5	16.0	14.0	11.0	15.0	13.91	14.50
A COMFORTABLE LIFE	12.0	14.0	12.0	12.0	16.0	11.0	12.83	12.00
A WORLD OF BEAUTY	18.0	15.0	13.0	15.5	15.0	13.0	14.91	15.00
AN EXCITING LIFE	15.0	16.5	18.0	15.5	17.0	17.0	16.50	16.75
PLEASURE	17.0	18.0	16.0	17.0	12.5	16.0	16.08	16.50
SOCIAL RECOGNITION	15.0	16.5	16.0	18.0	12.5	18.0	16.00	16.25

Kendall's W .89   Chi-Square 90.86 p < .0001

Table 4

GRADUATE STUDENTS' YEARLY RANKING OF INSTRUMENTAL VALUES
1983-88

	1983	1984	1985	1986	1987	1988	MEAN	MEDIAN
HONEST	2.0	1.0	1.0	1.0	1.0	1.0	1.16	1.00
LOVING	4.5	2.5	2.0	3.0	6.0	3.0	3.50	3.00
HELPFUL	12.0	6.0	5.0	10.5	5.0	9.0	7.91	7.50
RESPONSIBLE	1.0	2.5	3.0	2.0	2.0	2.0	2.08	2.00
BROADMINDED	9.0	7.5	6.0	10.5	13.0	10.0	9.33	9.50
FORGIVING	11.0	4.0	4.0	4.0	3.0	7.0	5.50	4.00
INDEPENDENT	6.0	9.0	7.0	6.0	12.0	6.0	7.66	6.50
COURAGEOUS	14.0	7.5	11.5	13.0	7.0	13.0	11.00	12.25
CAPABLE	4.5	5.0	9.0	5.0	4.0	4.0	5.25	4.75
INTELLECTUAL	3.0	10.0	11.5	8.0	9.0	5.0	7.75	8.50
IMAGINATIVE	13.0	16.5	13.5	16.0	15.0	15.0	14.83	15.00
SELF-CONTROLLED	7.0	12.0	8.0	12.0	8.0	12.0	9.83	10.00
CHEERFUL	15.0	13.0	10.0	9.0	17.0	11.0	12.50	12.00
LOGICAL	10.0	16.5	15.0	14.0	11.0	14.0	13.41	14.00
POLITE	16.0	14.0	13.5	15.0	18.0	17.0	15.58	15.50
AMBITIOUS	8.0	11.0	16.0	7.0	10.0	8.0	10.00	9.00
OBEDIENT	18.0	18.0	17.5	18.0	14.0	18.0	17.25	18.00
CLEAN	17.0	15.0	17.5	17.0	16.0	16.0	16.41	16.50

Kendall's W .84   Chi-Square 85.12 $p < .0001$

CHAPTER FIVE

THE NEW MORAL EDUCATION AND THESE USE OF RELATIVISM: A PRAGMATIC RESPONSE

by

Winston Bridges
University of South Florida
St. Petersburg

The purpose of this paper will be to explore selected, recent criticisms of schooling, the effort made to accomplish the moral education of the young and the uses of the term, moral or ethical and cultural relativism.

We should acknowledge Dewey's now obvious notion, lest someone bring it up, that almost all of schooling is pregnant with moral possibility.[1] Indeed, effective moral education would probably be thoroughly integrated into most school activities and would not be noticeable as a thing in itself. However, specific moral education techniques were developed and promoted during the 1960s and 1970s. Criticism of values clarification and Kohlberg's moral reasoning approach is nothing new. Much of the writing on the subject in the 1970s is devoted to just that. I assume that it is not necessary to detail these criticisms or to explain how these approaches work.

I would like to note that many of the allegations made during this period do include the charge that these techniques are susceptible to the problem of moral relativism. The case seems easily made with values clarification where individuals should be clear about their own values. The problem is supposed to be that students are encouraged to decide moral matters without necessary reference to moral principle, rationality or to others and that anything goes. Defenses have been made which observe that values clarification usually occurs in a social context where consequences are tested and that there are traditional values which are encouraged.[2] The charge is not so easily made against Kohlberg's moral reasoning. Various critics have argued that this approach encourages both an "objectivist Kantian Idealism" or a "contentless" skepticism about traditional western values.[3,4] Other papers will have to resolve this dispute.

In this paper I am concerned with the issue of relativism and how recent critics have used this notion. In general, it seems that in the 1980s a number of critics have argued that schooling and moral education have failed because of moral or ethical relativism and, more to the point, what is needed as a solution is an education which directly transmits "the virtues" or the "Western Philosophical Tradition" to form desirable character in our young. To these authors, self-centered, egoistic relativism has been our problem and objectivism imposed will, at least, improve the education of the young and may help correct the drift and chaos of a too permissive society where distinctions between right and wrong are never clear enough.

A partial example of this can be seen in an editorial written in "American Educator" (1980) by our unabashed former Secretary of Education, William J. Bennett. He attacks "values educationists" not as fomenters of ethical relativism, but as those who indoctrinate while claiming that indoctrination is the "most awful thing in the world." Bennett says these hypocritical educationists are biased in favor of inarticulate "left-wing communitarian or right-wing libertarian or trendy or Woodstockian" ideologies which he does not describe in any detail. However, the image of a subjectivistic/relativistic individualism or subculturism is produced. Furthermore, he says students are led to always put the burden or proof on authority and social convention with narrowly constructed exercises that emphasize decision-making. This does not lead to the really important part of morality which, for Bennett, is the development of character. The concept of character is not well developed but is related to "dispositions and habits of mind and heart." Bennett's preferred moral education technique is indicated when he writes about what teachers ought to be doing. He writes:

> It is certainly wrong to tell teachers not to tell students what their opinions are at appropriate times and not to tell students what they think they should do. That is why teachers have entered the profession in the first place--because they thought they could make a positive difference in the lives of students. Why must

teachers, who have the students' best interests at stake, be silenced? Why are they to silence themselves when the rest of the world--people outside the school, pushers, street corner flakes, etc.--are not similarly muzzled? If we stop teaching values, the task will simply pass to others....There are things of value to be learned from the reflections, judgements, and opinions of men and women of principle; however, there are blessings from teaching from indoctrination in the form of adults talking to children and telling them what they know and believe.[5]

Therefore, it would seem that moral education can be improved by teachers indoctrinating students to accept conventional virtue to form character. Bennett's polemic is really significant, not for logic or complexity, but because of his visibility and popular impact. His advocacy of character indoctrination and disparagement of so-called educationists may be hallmarks of the "new" moral education.

Edward A. Wynne offers an analysis that is similar to Bennett's. He reviews the values clarification and Kohlbergian efforts of the 1960s and finds them lacking for a number of reasons. One problem is a disavowal of concern with proper conduct in moral education. Proper conduct is supplanted by an emphasis on reasoning or feeling when right behavior ought to be the main business of good moral education. The lack of interest in proper conduct is fueled by an anti-indoctrination stance taken by these educators which, to Wynne, is wrong-headed and ultimately confusing. Wynne's position is that..."school is and should and must be inherently indoctrinative."[6] Since children do not know what they need to know and how to behave, we may view values clarification and Kohlberg's moral reasoning as ineffective. Indeed, Wynne points to dramatic increases in rates of youth homicide, suicide and illegitimate births to indicate the current dismal state of affairs and to discredit these techniques. Furthermore, Wynne devotes most of his effort in describing what he calls the "Great Tradition in Education," that is, the transmitting of moral values.

The "Great Tradition" is concerned with good habits of conduct as contrasted with moral concepts or moral rationales. In other words, good moral education is character education and consists of requiring, rewarding and punishing various behaviors since children are not capable of objectively assessing the beliefs and values they should have as adults. The basis for Wynne's "common sense" or conventional view of moral education is traditional culture.

Less the conservative ideologue than Bennett, and much more sophisticated than Wynne, Alan Bloom presents a more rational and reasoned critique of American culture and education in his best-selling book, The Closing of the American Mind. Bloom's success in the market place gives high visibility to traditional Platonic objectivism that deplores a rampant relativism which, to Bloom is cultural and not really distinguishable from an ethical or moral sort. Cultural relativism is our major problem. It produces a required openness that leads to a superficial sameness of mind. Bloom writes that:

> Actually openness results in American conformism--out there in the rest of the world is a drab diversity that teaches only that values are relative, whereas here we can create all the life-styles we want. Our openness means we do not need others. Thus, what is advertised as a great opening is a great closing. No longer is there a hope that there are great wise men in other places and times who can reveal the truth about life....[7]

Bloom's point seems to be that we now are so devoted to cultural tolerance or the acceptance of difference that we are unwilling and unable to judge the true and the good. He goes on:

> Openness used to be the virtue that permitted us to seek the good by using reason. It now means accepting everything and denying reason's power. The unrestrained and thoughtless pursuit of openness, without recognizing the inherent political, social, or

cultural problems of openness as the goal of nature, has rendered openness meaningless. Cultural relativism destroys one's own [meaning] and the good.[8]

Bloom's book goes on and develops these themes. His preference in education echoes Hutchins and Adler from fifty years before. He calls for a return to the classics, the Great Books, and particularly Plato's Republic which he extols as "the book on education" because it explains the possibility of a real community of men as those who seek after truth.[9] Then moral education to Bloom would occur with a return to the substantial tradition of western philosophy.

A similar view is seen in an article by Christana Hoff Sommers. She writes that values clarification and Kohlberg's moral reasoning approach have been dominant and they are wrong because they emphasize how and not what. And they certainly avoid the what of western literature and history. These techniques produce entering college students who are unencumbered by the "old bag of virtues," but who have a new rapbag which contains the following:

> psychological egoism (the belief that the primary motive for action is selfishness), moral relativism (the doctrine that what is praiseworthy or contemptible is a matter of cultural conditioning) and radical tolerance (the doctrine that to be culturally and socially aware is to understand and excuse the putative wrongdoer). Another item in the bag is the conviction that the seat of moral responsibility is found in society and its institutions, not in individuals.[10]

These students, to Sommers, lack common sense and many are thoroughly confused about morality. What is needed are "...some straightforward courses in moral philosophy and a sound and unabashed introduction to the western moral tradition."[11] But fear of indoctrination may prevent this. What has happened lately is a flourishing of applied ethics courses on college campuses which is better than nothing and may shake confidence in moral relativism. Applied ethics courses do have their drawbacks. They are oriented to issues and institutions without proper attention to individual responsibility and virtue. To Sommers, as with Bloom, true moral education can be achieved by having the student strive toward objective virtue as revealed by traditional western philosophy.

The New Moral Education

Is this the "new" moral education of the late 1980s? Are we moving in the direction of a traditional objectivism whether its base is in culture or tradition itself or some other world of truth? These are certainly open questions, but I would suggest there are more advocates of this general direction now speaking and publishing in the popular and professional press. Other examples can be seen in the writings of respected students of education such as Jonas Soltis who warns of "ethical subjectivism" and as a solution encourages us to accept the NEA "Code of Ethics." The Code is seen as a good one that represents a "telos" or purpose to which professionals should submit.[12] Another author, Kevin Ryan, has written about what he calls "The New Moral Education" which is based on the "five E's" of example, explanation, exhortation, environment and experience. I will not detail the approach, but it does praise character formation, Durkheim, teacher modeling and exhortation for moral excellence.[13]

I do not want to attempt a thorough analysis of any particular version of this new moral education here. There are important questions about the role of reason and indoctrination, about how alternative moral notions are considered if at all and the educational effectiveness of such direct approaches. Indeed, these questions have been raised and dealt with by others. We might note that the arguments made by the new moral education may point to some real problems in the "old" moral education of the 1960s and 1970s. Was there a sufficient emphasis on reason versus feeling? Was there a sensible link between thought and action or behavior? Is there a contribution to be made by a study of ethical theory or by metaethical reflection? The answers to these questions deserve consideration.

My purpose has been to review how the argument for the new moral education has been made. One prominent feature of that argument is to raise the specter of subjectivism/relativism in order to establish the problem to be overcome by traditional moral teaching. In general, the problem is that individuals are without sufficient standards for making moral judgements and they are left dissatisfied, confused or, at worst, narcissistic while social interests, true knowledge and virtue are ignored. The support for this criticism of subjectivsm/relativism ranges from the reasoned and lengthy as in Bloom to the terse and emotive in Bennett.

A Conceptual Framework

A conceptual framework from which to view this argument is offered by Adler. In __Ten Philosophical Mistakes__, Adler tells us that there are only two groups that dispute over moral values. There is one group that believes that moral values are "subjective and relative" on the one hand and on the other hand another group that believes that moral values are "objective and absolute." The subjective varies from one person to another and the relative varies in time and circumstance. The error committed by this view, simply put, is that if subjectivism/relativism allows claims to the good to be based on different individuals, times or circumstances, then there is no way to resolve competing or conflicting claims. Adler goes on to "prove," in his own mind, an objective and absolute moral truth by overcoming the fact/value distinction through assuming, with Aristotle, that there is a truth in practical judgement where normative judgements are joined with action. These practical judgements must conform with what our nature requires. Our desires should be natural and related to our needs. Finally, "we ought to desire whatever is really good for us and nothing else" becomes the first principle in moral philosophy.[14]

I think this is much more of Adler than we really need. One can argue with his assumptions about practical judgement and natural desires or needs and where all this may lead. My interest here is in showing the conceptual framework which is essentially bipolar where one view is easily dispatched and the other is established without much difficulty. This approach appears to be used by the proponents of the new moral education as well as by Adler. One might wonder if there are other alternatives and how many? Is there a simplistic grouping that takes place here? I think the answer is yes.

In closing, I would like to consider one other alternative which is advocated by Kenneth Howe. That is, fallibilism which is both rational, pluralistic and allows uncertainty and disagreement. Howe's conceptual framework is an improvement. It offers three positions. Fallibilism lies between absolutism and subjectivism. According to Howe:

> Absolutists point to clear examples at the non-controversial end of the spectrum of moral beliefs; for example, it is wrong to torture children for the fun of it. They generalize that all moral beliefs enjoy the same level of certitude and conclude that anyone who disagrees with them is wrong (or worse). Subjectivists, by contrast, point to clear examples at the highly controversial end of the spectrum; for example, abortion is morally wrong. They generalize that all moral beliefs must be equally uncertain and conclude that moral beliefs are simply a matter of subjective tastes and preferences. Both of these extreme views leave ethical inquiry at an impasse, and both views are open to criticism. [15]

Howe says that absolutists have problems with democratic values such as freedom of religion and the exchange of ideas while subjectivists have difficulty showing the point in any ethical discourse and how reason might apply. And both are guilty of over-generalizing. "Fallibilism asserts that there are many cases in between these extremes where careful inquiry..." is valued and disagreement as well as uncertainty may continue. Fallibilism places critical reflection at the center of ethical inquiry and, in this, is seen as in accord with Dewey, Peters, Scheffler and Scriven. Howe's fallibilism does contain more elements than we can explore here, however, we can focus on the role of rationality. The teacher in an ethics course is to employ rational criticism, Socratic questioning, where distinctions are required in positions taken, alternatives are considered, reasons offered, consequences are tested and logic is applied.

The relationship between Howe's fallibilism and ethical theory (either normative or applied) is one where such theories may be useful on occasion to inform, but are "kept in the background and broached only if the need arises." Howe worries about the use of these theories in teacher education. Even applied theories such as values clarification or Kohlbergian notions can be applied mechanically and with greater authority than is deserved. The fallibilist concern with critical reflection means that all theories or ideas should be scrutinized carefully.

As with many papers like this, more questions are raised (either directly or implicitly) than are answered. Howe's fallibilism which seems well within the tradition of pragmatism is an attempt to reassert a reasoned alternative to objectivist or subjectivist theories of moral education. Critiques by proponents of objectivism or subjectivism seldom include close scrutiny of fallibilistic notions and may simply lump fallibilism together with their opposite. In the case of the so-called "new moral education," fallibilistic notions are likely to be seen as subjectivistic/relativistic and then dismissed as unworthy. Is fallibilism likely to lead to ethical relativism where confusion reigns or a more profoundly held sense of what should be done than could be accomplished by indoctrinative approaches? I hope it is the latter.

The pragmatist, Richard Rorty, believes that there are really no relativists. For no one believes that two incompatible opinions about an important topic are equally good. The real issue, to Rorty, is "...not between people who think one view is as good as another and people who do not. It is between those who think our culture, or purpose, or intuitions cannot be supported except conversationally, and people who still hope for other sorts of support."[16] Rorty writes that the reflective mind is confronted with a fundamental choice:

> that between accepting the contingent character of starting points, and attempting to evade this contingency. To accept the contingency of starting-points is to accept our inheritance from, and our conversation with, our fellow-humans as our only source of guidance. To attempt to evade this

contingency is to hope to become a properly-programmed machine. This was the hope...that might (it) be fulfilled by finding the a priori structure of any possible inquiry, or language, or form of social life. If we give up this hope, we shall lose what Nietzsche called "metaphysical comfort," but we may gain a renewed sense of community. Our identification...is heightened when we see this community as ours rather than nature's, shaped rather than found, one among many which men have made. In the end, the pragmatists tell us, what matters is our loyalty to other human beings clinging together against the dark, not our hope of getting things right.[17]

FOOTNOTES

1. John Dewey, Moral Principles in Education (Carbondale: University of Illinois Press, 1975).

2. James J. Brummer, "Moralizing and the Philosophy of Value Education," The Educational Forum, 48 (Winter, 1984).

3. Christina Hoff Sommers, "Ethics Without Virtue: Moral Education in America," The American Scholar 53.

4. Allan L. Lockwood, "Keeping Them in the Courtyard: A Response to Wynne," Educational Leadership, 43, No. 4 (Dec. 85/Jan. 86) pp. 9-10.

5. William J. Bennett, "What is Values Education?" American Educator, 8, No. 3 (Fall, 1980) pp. 31-32.

6. Edward A. Wynne, "The Great Tradition in Education: Transmitting Moral Values," Educational Leadership, 43, No. 4 (Dec. 85/Jan. 86) p. 9.

7. Allan Bloom, The Closing of the American Mind. (New York: Simon and Schuster, 1987) p. 34.

8. Bloom, p. 38.

9. Bloom, p. 381.

10. Sommers, p. 386.

11. Sommers, p. 387.

12. Jonas F. Soltis, "Teaching Professional Ethics," Journal of Teacher Education, 37, No. 3 (May-June 1986) pp. 2-4.

13. Kevin Ryan, "The New Moral Education," Phi Delta Kappan, 68, No. 4 (November, 1986) pp. 228-233.

14. Mortimer J. Adler, Ten Philosophical Mistakes (New York: Macmillan, 1985).

15. Kenneth R. Howe, "A Conceptual Basis for Ethics in Teacher Education," Journal of Teacher Education, 37, No. 3 (May-June 1986) p. 7.

16. Richard Rorty, Consequences of Pragmatism (Essays: 1972-1980) (Minneapolis: University of Minnesota Press, 1982).

17. Rorty, p. 166.

CHAPTER FIVE

CHANCE METAPHYSICS AND EDUCATION

by

Kenneth D. McCracken
University of Tennessee, Martin

For many persons, the word "metaphysics" conjures up memories of propositions that attempt to solve such problems as how many angels can dance on the head of a pin or what is the function of the navel.[1] Metaphysics is often believed to belong to the trashheap of useless medieval studies along with the Ptolemaic model of the Universe or the phlogiston theory of burning. Some professors are as quick to state that they are non-metaphysical as some ministers are to state that they are non-theological. But this denial appears to me to be no more than an escape mechanism.

Perhaps some persons would rather believe that their metaphysical concepts are some eternal truth rather than philosophical speculation, and the word "metaphysics" strikes a blow at their belief system. And they do have a valid point if they believe this. Metaphysical views can never be verified by scientific experiment; in fact, these views are so loose that it is impossible even to demonstrate that they are false. From the standpoint of verification, these concepts merely "sit there," subject to approval, disapproval or neglect, whichever suits the fancy of the individual who hears it.

Nonetheless, it is a serious mistake to consider these untestable concepts as mere mental creations that generate neither activity nor events. Far from being a mental exercise suitably only to pedantics, metaphysics is, instead, an everyday phenomenon which operates in the kitchen and the classroom. If anything is missing, it is the use of the word "metaphysics."

The Puritan fathers operationalized a number of their metaphysical beliefs such as their belief that the child was conceived in sin and born in sin--they practiced this particular concept by beating the Devil out of them. This is not the only deduction that can be developed by the "born-in-sin" concept. A minister friend of mine who had this belief had a child who was more spoiled than mine; evidently, he believed that one should love the Devil out of them.

B. F. Skinner has stated in Science and Human Behavior that an assumption that man is not free is necessary for the development of a science of human behavior.[2] Many physicists on the other hand claim that molecules, if not free, are certainly unpredictable. And it is difficult to find anyone who has developed better scientific principles than have the physicists. Yet during the Nineteenth Century, most physicists had a philosophical view similar to Skinner's. Under the realistic, natural law, cause-and-effect concept, all phenomena would eventually be known, and predictions would be virtually one hundred per cent correct. As James Jeans has stated, there was a time when physicists believed they were to the point of working out a few more decimal places, dotting the i's and crossing the t's.[3] The metaphysics of physics has since then evolved into a chance pattern that was so unordered that it has prompted physicists to search for a new form of order.[4]

Sometime during my teens, I discovered that there were views of the Universe based on disorder. Also I learned of beliefs that many of the mathematical concepts that I labored so hard to learn had no reality at all and that such constructs as circles and straight lines had no existence except in somebody's head. Later, I became puzzled by the academic separation of mathematics and statistics since, to me, they looked so much alike. The differences were not that primarily of content. Mathematics, historically, has developed by the principles of Pythagorean and Platonic idealism, and statistics developed by methods of utilitarianism, pragmatism, and experimentalism. In mathematics, most propositions could be proved by the principle of deductive reasoning on a truth-to-truth basis. Statistics, the science of the gambling hall, had no such self-evident truths. The statistician could only develop categories and collect data, and hopefully generalize from these data. The centuries of statistics had taught one great generalization above all others; viz. one can predict the mass better than the individual. It was almost as if that order comes out of chaos and the more the chaos the more the order (chaos must of course have the proper operational definition for this to be accurate).

I would admit that an unordered Universe did not appeal to me as a young person. I had been taught one form of order in church and another form in most, not all, of my science and math classes. But, in Vaihinger's language, I acted as if I believed in disordered, chance environment.[5] It was quite obvious in games that I played, and probably less obvious in decisions I made concerning occupations and schooling.

The predictability of the masses, as opposed to the unpredictability of the individual became focused when I was assigned a job as a part-time counselor in high school. During the Fifties, it was almost fashionable for students to want an interpretation of their standardized test scores along with advice of what they should do. I was always bothered when students asked me for these interpretations. In some instances, these tests did have considerable validity, e.g., IQ and GPA often would show a validity of something like .60. For a group, it is accurate to state that such tests were certainly useful if not particularly accurate. But the job of the high school counselor is far different from that of the personnel director. The latter, if he were trying to improve the quality of the work force, could use such tests profitably. Though he might miss a few gems and permit some less-then-gems to work, the average worker (an obvious hypothetical construct) would be enhanced. In his case, he was working for the company, not the worker. As a counselor, however, I was interested only in the person who was in my office. To counsel one person on the basis of a battery of tests was far different than estimating the achievement level of the school on the basis of such a battery. The error factor of the test became very important. This student might be the exception rather than the rule and I had to consider this factor.

This unpredictability of individuals reinforced my belief that each individual was unique; it is only with groups that one can generalize concepts about characteristics of groups such as teenagers.

If people are unpredictable and individualists it follows (with apologies for the deductive logic) that teaching methods can be no more than a starting point of a teaching style. It follows that teachers would seek their own methods and approaches to learning if they have enough flexibility and enough caring to do.

This theory of chance perhaps forces one to develop another hypothesis--people, operating through their minds--have the power to de-randomize as well as to create. Order, then is a function of people, and this order can be used to develop diversity as well as convergence.

Education can never be the same for everyone (with apologies to Mortimer Adler). We are too unpredictable for that; thank God for that unpredictability.

FOOTNOTES

1. S. Samuel Shermis, Philosophic foundations of Education. (New York: Van Nostrand Reinhold Company, 1967). On page 44-46 under a heading, "The History of an Unpopular Subject," he states an opinion of that beliefs about metaphysics that is similar to that found in this paper. He does not use the navel cliche however.

2. B. F. Skinner, Science and Human Behavior, (New York: The Free Press, Macmillan Publishing Co., Inc., 1953). He states "We cannot apply the methods of science to a subject matter which is assumed to move about capriciously." Where would physics be now if they followed this principle?

3. Sir James Jeans, The Growth of Physical Science. (Greenwich, Conn.: Fawcett Publications, Inc., 1958). (originally published by Cambridge University Press, 1947), p. 257. It is questionable that Jeans, although he might practice indeterminacy and related concepts, could accept this chance model as an actual model of the Universe.

4. Bryan Bunch (Ed.) The Science Almanac, 1985-86 Edition, (Garden City, N.Y.: Anchor Press/Doubleday, 1984). On pages 515-17 is a discussion of Grand Unification Schemes. It is possible that one of these may provide an orderly Universe.

5. Hans Vaihinger, The Philosophy of the As If. (New York: Harcourt Brace Company, 1925).

BIBLIOGRAPHY

Bunch, Bryan (Ed.) The Science Almanac, 1985-86 Edition. Garden City, N.Y.: Anchor Press/Doubleday, 1984, pp. 515-17.

Jeans, James Sir. The Growth of Physical Science. Greenwich, Conn.: Fawcett Publications, Inc., 1958 (originally published by Cambridge University Press, 1947), p. 257.

Shermis, Samuel S. Philosophic Foundations of Education. New York: Van Nostrand Reinhold Company, 1967, pp. 44-46.

Skinner, B. F. Science and Human Behavior. New York: The Free Press, Macmillan Publishing Co., Inc., 1953.

Vaihinger, Hans. The Philosophy of the As If. New York: Harcourt Brace Company, 1925.

CHAPTER FIVE

RECENT DEVELOPMENTS IN QUANTUM PHYSICS AND
THEIR IMPLICATIONS FOR PHILOSOPHY OF
EDUCATION: IS THERE CONDITIONAL DETERMINISM?

by

Donald L. Grigsby
University of Alabama, Birmingham

The purpose of this paper is threefold, first to discuss recent developments in quantum physics coming from the work of Alain Aspect and his colleagues at the University of Paris' Institute of Theoretical and Applied Optics in Orsay. A second purpose is to place the results of this work in historical context. The final purpose is to suggest that the results of this work will have an impact on the philosophy of education as it is found on American college and university campuses. Before discussing Aspect's work, it is necessary to look at some of the constructs found in quantum physics.

CONSTRUCTS

The first construct is that of the levels of physics. A primary level of course is that which is commonly called classical physics. This is the mechanistic realm where phenomena are still predictable, where there is a marked degree of determinism and where objective reality still seems to exist. A second level of physics is the quantum realm; here problems begin to arise. Phenomena are no longer as predictable. Particle behavior is more statistical in nature. At this level determinism is no longer viable and objective reality is doubtful. Finally, the question arises, is there another level of physics below the quantum level? Asked another way, are there hidden variables in the quantum realm which, if discovered, would lead to another level of physics?

A second construct is that of non-local effects. Basically, the question is; do non-local effects exist? That is, are there influences between particles, when they are so far apart that the effect can not be explained. These non-local effects have been called faster than light communications. They have also been called spooky actions at a distance and they bothered Einstein (Zukav, 288). One of the best descriptions of the non-local effect is found in the book Taking the Quantum Leap by Fred Alan Wolf. He describes this spooky action at a distance in the realm of our knowledge and observation. Suppose you have a bottle of champagne. When your bottle was filled, there were several others filled at the same time, and you bought only one of them. The rest of the bottles are elsewhere, non-local to you. It now comes time to open your bottle and nothing happens to the other bottles. However, if non-local effects exist, you open your bottle and all of the others bottled at the same time lose some of their carbonation. Not only do they lose some of their carbonation, they all lose it instantaneously as soon as you open your bottle (Wolf, 202-4). That sounds spooky and is exactly the problem. To test for this spookyness at the quantum level was one of the purposes of Aspect's work.

Thirdly, there is the construct of the nature of reality. Is there an objective reality or is the physical existence of a particle dependent upon the observer and his observation of it? In classical physics there is the old question of a tree falling in the forest. If there is no one around to hear it, is there any sound? Classically we would say that there needs to be a receptor for there to be sound and so by definition no sound is there. But the question of reality goes farther than that. In the quantum sense, there will not even be any sound waves unless there is an observer there to create them by his observation. A good example of this is found in the article, "Is the moon there when nobody looks? Reality and the quantum theory," by David Mermin (Mermin, 38). Does the observer merely find reality or does he create reality? Is there a physical reality "out there" to be discovered or is there a subjective reality to be created? The essence of this construct is implicit in the Aspect work.

Finally, there is the construct of determinism. In classical physics, we find that, for all practical purposes, one event can determine another. The paths of two pool balls are determined by the way they collide with each other. At the quantum level, however, such determinism is doubtful. If such determinism were to exist measurement of it is questionable, if not impossible. Further, because of the nature of the quantum realm only probable individual events occur, not certain individual events (Wolf, 104).

HISTORICAL PERSPECTIVE

With these constructs in mind, it is necessary to put Aspect's work in historical perspective. One of the first events was the Heisenberg Uncertainty Principle. In this principle, Heisenberg shows that when a particle has two quantities, position and momentum, both properties cannot be determined exactly and simultaneously (Zukav, 111). Since both properties cannot be measured, the one that is chosen is the one which the observer creates. There are at least two different views on the existence of the other property. One is that the property exists but is just not being measured. The more extreme position is that the property doesn't exist at all and will never exist until the observer chooses to measure it. This latter position is most common in quantum interpretation of reality (Mermin, 40-41).

The next event in this history came from the Einstein, Podosky, Rosen paper, in 1935. In this paper the authors proposed a thought experiment that dealt with two particles instead of one in the Heisenberg Uncertainty Principle. Classically, if two pool balls collide, what is happening to one ball can be determined by observing the other one after the collision. The EPR paper did not have particles colliding with each other, instead, particles were allowed to collide with a barrier with two slits in it. Two particles get through the slits and are observed. If the momentum of one particle is measured, then the momentum of the other particle will be known. If the position of one of the particles is measured, then the position of the other particles will be known. In a quantum sense, measurement of one particle creates reality for the other particle (Wolf, 159). This is the spooky action at a distance. What is done at one location causes reality at another location instantaneously. This is like the champagne in the bottle described above. Why this should happen is not clear. Some have called it communication beyond the speed of light and others have called it a "mystical" process. Regardless of what it is, it is the spooky action at a distance and Einstein could not accept it. He therefore assumed that quantum physics was incomplete and that hidden variables existed (Zukav, 285). In essence, he theorized that there was another realm of physics below the quantum level. This had kept the physics world in discussion for years trying to reconcile these assertions. Aspect and his colleagues have provided some conclusive data in this area.

Another chapter in the continuing saga of quantum physics and reality comes from John Bell and his theorem. In 1964 Bell was working on the problems of the EPR interpretation of non-local effects and eventually published his paper (Mermin, 40). In summary, Bell concludes that if there are hidden variables such as the EPR position claims, that such variables cannot be local, instead they must be non-local. In essence, Bell shows that if there are hidden variables and they are local in nature, then they would obviate the observable results of quantum physics. We know the success of quantum physics in areas such as transistors, superconductivity and a host of other areas. So, Bell concludes that hidden variables do exist, that they are not local, rather they are non-local (Wolf, 293). Partial experimental confirmation of Bell's theorem came from the work of John Clauser and his colleagues at the Lawrence Berkeley Laboratory in 1972. These experimental results, however, lacked conclusive confirmation (Zukav, 293-4) which the work of Aspect and his colleagues appears to provide.

ASPECT EXPERIMENT

In the experiment described by Mermim in his article, Aspect uses calcium atoms excited by a laser. The remitted photons are then directed 180 degrees from each other to receivers where their polarization is observed. The receivers are far enough apart, 12 to 13 meters, to make any effects non-local. A Sterm-Gerlach magnet switches the north pole to one of the three directions, 120 degrees apart. (See Figure 1 for a simple diagram of the apparatus.)

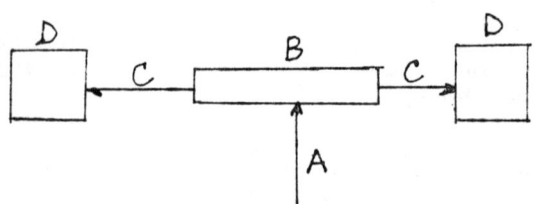

Figure 1. Simple diagram of experimental apparatus: (A) Laser light, (B) Calcium Atoms, (C) Reemitted Photons, (D) Receivers

To make the experiment more understandable, Mermin sets up a classical diagram, Figure 2.

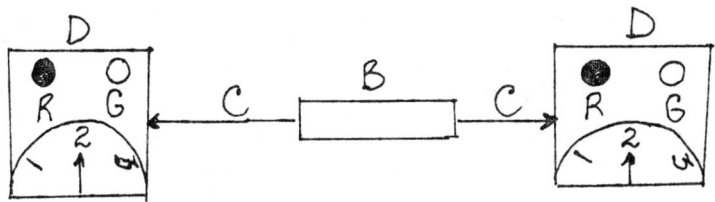

Figure 2. Classical representation of the experimental apparatus, showing 22RR run.

At B he has the source of the photons and at D he has the receptors. The switches 1, 2, and 3 correspond to the three directions of the magnetic north pole and will always be set randomly. Finally, the polarization of the photon is represented by red and green colored lights. When the lights are the same color, that represents the photons having the same polarization.

In the runs of the experiment the switches at each of the receptors are set randomly, then the color of the lights is observed. The resultant data take the following form: 13RG, 21GR, 22RR, 32RG, 31GG, 11GG, 12RG, 33GG. As is expected, the colors at each of the receptors will be green half the time and red half the time. To have the lights the same at both receivers, RR or GG, this will occur one-fourth of the time. The switch settings on each of the receptors will be 1 one-third of the time, 2 one-third of the time and 3 one-third of the time and that is observed. Likewise there will be identical switch settings, 11, 22, and 33. What was not expected was that when the switch settings were the same, 11, 22, or 33, then the lights were always the same color. There could be identical light colors with different switch setting, but there was no identical switch settings without identical colors. These results are the bases for the importance of the data. Does this confirm the spooky action at a distance? Does it imply a realm of physics below the quantum level? Does it refute the EPR position and confirm the Bell Theorem? These questions are well beyond the scope of this paper, but what does appear to be certain is that there will now be a new series of philosophical implications as a result of these data.

PHILOSOPHICAL IMPLICATIONS

A thorough discussion of these philosophical implications cannot be treated in the limited scope of this paper. However, it appears that there are at least two philosophical interpretations of these data which can be suggested. First, those who have opted for the "mystical" interpretation of quantum physics will find in these data support for their position. These results will probably be interpreted as mystic communication and the full spectrum of the new age movements will welcome such an interpretation. These movements have gained momentum over the past few years and data such as these appear to be fertile ground for these groups. Further, groups such as these along with certain oriental mystical groups have been quite active on American college and university campuses. Thus the impact of the Aspect results seem to already have a path to our students.

A second interpretation of these data can be found in the position suggested in the title of this paper; is there a conditional determinism? This position is in direct opposition to many interpreters of quantum physics. Regardless of how offensive this position might be, it at least appears that when the switches are the same, (11, 22, 33) then the lights will be the same (GG or RR). In short, if the switches are alike, then the lights are alike and a conditional determinism can be posited. Neither of these positions was suggested by Mermin in his article, nor have either of these positions been found in the literature. They are merely interpretations of the data from Aspect's work. Knowing how college and university students think, based on years of teaching courses in philosophy of education, these two interpretations can be expected from students on our college and university campuses.

Finally, we have seen the impact of quantum physics on western philosophy for over fifty years. Zukav even goes so far as to make a direct connection between the Copenhagen interpretation and pragmatism (Zukav, 38). If such an assertion is founded, and since there is such close connection between Pragmatism and our American schools, the impact of the Aspect experiments is not to be taken lightly.

BIBLIOGRAPHY

Mermin, N. David, "Is the Moon there when nobody looks? Reality and the quantum theory." <u>Physics Today</u>, April 1985, 38-47.

Wolf, Fred Alan, <u>Taking the Quantum Leap</u>, San Francisco, Harper & Row, Publishers, 1981.

Zukav, Gary, <u>The Dancing Wu Li Masters</u>, New york: Bantom Books, 1979.

CHAPTER SIX

THERE'S A POT 'A BREWIN' IN PSYCHOLOCIGAL RESEARCH METHODOLOGY: WHAT DOES IT MEAN FOR RESEARCH IN EDUCATION

by

Michael A. Orey
James W. Garrison
John K. Burton
Virginia Polytechnic Institute
and State University

Introduction

During the past two decades, there has been a continuing philosophical debate over the research methodology apropos for psychology in particular and the utility of null hypothesis testing in general. The controversy began with Meehl's (1967, 1978) Popperian critique of psychology's research methodology. Serlin and Lapsley (1985) countered by appealing to the philosophy of science of Imre Lakatos (1978a, 1978b). Dar (1987) provides the most recent (and to some degree most synthetic) entry when he rebutts Serlin and Lapsley's article in terms of Lakatos' interpretation of psychology as a science. One wonders if this debate is just a tempest in a tea pot, or whether something is brewing in all this turmoil that educational researchers should attend to? Certainly if Meehl's critique holds up it may be readily extended to include a number of the social sciences that impinge prominently on education and are important areas of educational research. This paper attempts to clarify this debate, bring it into the arena of educational research, and show why it is far from settled.

Meehl's Point of View

Meehl (1967, 1978) critiques the heavy dependence upon the statistical techniques of R. A. Fisher (1967) in the testing of psychological theory in those areas he designates as "soft psychology." Meehl is particularly concerned with the methodology and underlying logic of null hypothesis testing. His concerns arise from the perspective of Popper's philosophy of science, within which the central idea is that the problem of inducation or confirmation is intractable. Popper points out that the logic of confirmation (i.e., E therefore T, where (T) is some theory and (E) some experimental or experiential evidence) is an invalid logical argument form commonly known as the fallacy of affirming the consequent. Popper concludes from this that "there is neither a psychologically nor a logical induction. Only the falsity of the theory can be inferred from empirical evidence, and this inference is a purely deductive one" (Popper, 1968, pp. 54-55). Popper certainly appears to have the weight of logic on his side. The logic refutation (i.e., E, not E therefore not T) is a logically valid argument form known as modus tollens. Popper concludes from this that all reasoning is either deductive or defective, and therefore the growth of science depends on a series of conjectures and refutations (See Garrison, 1986, p. 13). Theories that survive a stiff test, i.e., are not refuted, are not said to be confirmed but rather "corroborated."

Following Popper, in order to effectively test a theory, the theory must be exposed to a serious risk of modus tollens refutation. Meehl contends that theories in soft psychology are rarely, if ever, threatened, much less placed in grave danger of refutation. One sad consequence of this situation, according to Meehl, is the slow pace of theoretical progress in soft psychology. As he puts it, "in fields like personology and social psychology" refutation does not occur; rather,

> There is a period of enthusiasm about a new theory, a period of attempted application to several fact domains, a period of disillusionment as negative data comes in, a growing bafflement about inconsistent and unreplicable empirical results, multiple resort to ad hoc excuses, and then finally people just sort of lose interest in the thing and pursue other endeavors. (Meehl, 1978, p. 807)

It is easy to see how Meehl arrives at his view given his Popperian predilections.

So what prevents theories in soft psychology and much of the social sciences from being exposed to the risk of refutation? Meehl gives several answers, but they all center around what he sees as an unfortunate reliance on Fisher's statistical methods, or more exactly, the reliance on null hypothesis testing.

One concern is that in the social sciences, unlike the physical sciences, there is no intimate connection between a substantive core theory (T) and the auxiliary constructs and theories (A) that tie the theory (T) to the experimental evidence (E). (As a consequence, psychometric instruments tend to be far more loosely connected to the constructs within the core theory than they are, for instance, in physics.) When we include auxiliary constructs and theories in the logic of modus tollens argumentation we obtain (T and A) E, $\overline{E}$, therefore (T and A) which is logically equivalent to $\overline{T}$ or $\overline{A}$. What this means is that some auxiliary or combination of auxiliaries may absorb the refutation leaving the substantive core theory untouched (See Garrison, 1986, p. 13). This logical possibility is the same in physics as in psychology, but in the former (A) is tightly connected to (T), often by logical derivability. As a result, a refutation is far more likely to penetrate the theoretical core in physics than in psychology. Substantive theories are, consequently, far more exposed to the risk of refutation. Further, because of the looseness of the nomological network connecting theory and experience in psychology, there is plenty of room to introduce ad hoc hypotheses in the guise of previously overlooked auxiliary theories, constructs of variables to explain the failure of a test. However important, these concerns are actually rather tangential to Meehl's deepest doubts about the propriety of the methodology of null hypothesis testing.

Meehl's primary concern is with a methodological puzzle so serious that he believes it deserves the designation "paradox." Meehl (1967) states the paradox in this way:

> In the physical sciences, the usual result of an improvement in experimental design, instrumentation, or numerical mass of data, is to increase the difficulty of the "observational hurdle" which the physical theory of interest must successfully surmount; whereas, in psychology and some of the allied behavior sciences, the usual effect of such improvement in experimental

precision is to provide an easier hurdle for the theory to surmount. (p. 103, Author's italics)

Among these "allied behavior sciences" are many of the social sciences that impinge in important ways upon the field of education.

Meehl ultimately traces the origin of this methodological paradox to the asymmetry between hypothesis testing in physics and the other hard sciences and null hypothesis testing in soft psychology and its allies. In physics we usually make an empirical prediction of a quantitative point-value, magnitude, or form function (complete with parameters to be fitted) derived from a substantive theory so that "improvements in the accuracy of determining this experimental function-form or point-value, whether by better instrumentation for control and making observations, or by the gathering of a larger number of measurements, has the effect of narrowing the band of tolerance about the theoretically predicted value" (Meehl, 1968, p. 112).

As a consequence of this narrowing band of tolerance about the predicted value or function form, the substantive theory becomes exposed to an ever increasing likelihood of refutation. In psychology by contrast, the researcher, on the basis of some psychological theory (T), "derives (often in a rather loose sense of 'derive') the consequence that an observable variable X will differ as between two groups of subjects" (Meehl, 1967, p. 104). We may write this generally as (i.e., the two groups are not equal) where a and b are any two arbitrary groups. This is the asymmetry. We do not test a predicted point value, rather we test the logical complement of the predicted outcome (i.e., that there is no difference between two subjects or variables). This, of course, is the "point-null" hypothesis (i.e.,).

One curious consequence of this asymmetry is that, unlike physics, the effect of better experimental design, improving experimental technique and instrumentation (along with enlarging sample size), is to <u>enhance</u> the likelihood of rejecting the point-null hypothesis. This <u>decreases</u> the likelihood of rejecting the theoretically <u>"derived"</u> prediction and the theory that gave rise to it. Indeed, Meehl argues, the point-null hypothesis is "quasi'always false" because "in order for two groups...to be <u>exactly</u> equal on such an output variable, we have to imagine that they are exactly equal <u>or</u> delicately counterbalanced on all of the contributors, which will never be the case." (Meehl, 1978, p. 822). "Putting it crudely," Meehl, (1978, p. 822) concludes "if you have enough cases and your measures are not totally unreliable, the null hypothesis will always be falsified, <u>regardless of the truth of the substantive theory</u> (author's atialics)."

Moreover, using urn theory, Meehl demonstrates that using the more common directional null hypothesis (i.e.,) the probability of rejecting the null is at least .50, given <u>no</u> substantive theory at all, and could be much higher given "strong" variables such as IQ, SES, etc. As a result meehl concludes that:

> ...the effect of increased precision, whether achieved by improved instrumentation and control, greater sensitivity in the logical structure of the experiment, or increasing the number of observations is to yield a probability approaching 1/2 of corroborating our substantive theory by a significant test, <u>even if the theory is totally without merit</u>. That is to say, the ordinary result of improving our experimental methods and increasing our sample size, proceeding in accordance with the traditionally accepted method of theory-testing by refuting a directional null hypothesis, yields a prior probability <u>p</u> ~ 1/2 and very likely somewhat above that value by an unknown amount. It goes without saying that successfully negotiating an experimental hurdle of this sort can constitute only an extremely weal corroboration of any substantive theory (Meehl, 1967, p. 111).

Meehl (1967) feels that the inadequate appreciation of the extreme weakness of the test to which a substantive theory T is subjected by null hypothesis testing and the resulting methodological asymmetry "is then compounded by a truly remarkable failure to recognize the logical asymmetry between... `confirmation' of a theory via affirming the consequent...and...the deductively tight refutation of a theory modus tollens...." (p. 112). The failure to recognize this logical asymmetry reinforces and compounds the errors that arise from the failure to recognize the methodological asymmetry or paradox. What disturbs Meehl most is that the social scientists' failure to recognize the logical force of modus tollens leads them to "treat disconfirming instances with equal methodological respect, as if one could, so to speak, 'count noses,' so that if a theory has somewhat more confirming instances, it is in pretty good shape evidentially" (Meehl, 1967, p. 112).

The belief that a theory is sound if there are only a few cases where it does not hold true seriously undermines the logical power of modus tollens. One ugly fact ought, at first glance, to be enough to falsify a theory. The theoretical proposition that "all swans are white" can survive any number of tests. Indeed, one could spend a lifetime finding confirming instances of white swanness. If, however, while visiting your Australian friend you are shown one black swan, and you have in your life seen 1,001 white swans, does it mean that the initial premise that, all swans are white, is weakened or is it simply proven wrong. Hmm! In psychological research and research reviews, Meehl argues that researchers merely add up positive and negative instances and if there are enough of the former and/or few enough of the latter they tend to conclude that the theory is pretty good or at least good enough.

Beyond the above mentioned reservations Meehl also bemoans the general absence of substantial theory to begin with and a tendency even by those who know better to conflate "the substantive theory of interest and the statistical hypothesis which is derived from it" (Meehl, 1967, p. 107).

Meehl's final conclusion is that there are five social forces and intellectual traditions at work in the behavior sciences which make the research consequences of this [paradoxical] situation even worse than they may have to be, considering the state of knowledge. In addition to (a) failure to recognize the marked asymmetry between confirmation and modus tollens refutation of theories, and (b) inadequate appreciation of the extreme weakness of the hurdle provide by the mere directional significance test, there exist among psychologists [and their allies], (c) a fairly widespread tendency to report experimental findings with a liberal use of ad hoc explanations for those that didn't 'pan out'.... The methodological price paid...is, of course, (d) an unusual ease of escape from modus tollens refutation....It is not unusual that (e) this ad hoc challenging of auxiliary hypotheses is repeated in the course of a series of related experiments.... In this fashion a zealous and clever investigator can slowly wend his way through a tenuous nomological network, performing a long series of related experiments which appear to the uncritical reader as a fine example of an integrated research program, without even once refuting or corroborating so much as a single strand of the network' (Meehl, 1967, pp. 113-114). Needless to say conclusions of methodological chicanery such as these cannot go unchallenged. What is remarkable is that we should have to wait nearly twenty years after Meehl's first critique before receiving Serlin and Lapsley's long overdue reply.

Serlin and Lapsley's Point of View

Serlin and Lapsley (1985) counter Meehl by resorting to the "sophisticated methodological falsification" of Popper's student, Imre Lakatos (1978a, 1978b). The difference between Lakatos' sophisticated, and Popper's so-called naive or dogmatic falsification, according to Serlin and Lapsley, is the recognition of the important role of auxiliary theories, constructs, et cetera that form a "protective belt" or negative heuristic around the "hard core" or positive heuristic of a theory or research program. The reason this protective belt of auxiliaries (A) exists is to tie theory (T) to the empirical test (E). Dogmatic falsificationists tend to ignore several interwoven problems in connecting theory to empirical facts. First, "what are considered facts are only acceptable to us if we believe in certain theories that describe how our measuring instruments work" (Serlin & Lapsley, 1985, p. 76). Second, "there can be no sensations unimpregnated by expectations, and therefore there is no natural demarcation between observational and theoretical propositions" (Lakatos, 1978a, p. 150. Third, "the potential falsifiers of a theory are granted 'observational' status by [methodological] decision" (Serlin & Lapsley, 1985, p. 76). As a consequence of all of this, Serlin and Lapsley (1985) conclude that "every scientific theory contains a ceteris paribus clause, so that it is a theory plus the ceteris paribus clause that is subjected to a test. Because it is always possible to replace the ceteris paribus clause, any simple test of a theory is of little consequence." (p. 76) (The ceteris paribus clause states that all things are assumed to be equal except those conditions actually manipulated.)

All of the above problems and concepts arise from the legion of auxiliaries needed to tie theory to test and all operate so as to mitigate the logical force of modus tollens refutation. Meehl (1978) fairly invites such a rejoinder. Indeed, he even mentions Lakatos (as well as Feyerabend) and conceded that: "I am not persuaded...that Sir Karl [Popper] adequately appreciates the degree in which this theory and auxiliary problem permeate research in inexact sciences, especially the social sciences...." (p. 821). By the "theory and auxiliary problem," Meehl means the difficulty of pinning the refutation upon some statement or conjunction of statements in the core theory and the ease with which the various auxiliary theories, constructs and variables (A) may properly protect a core theory (T) from refutation.

As a result of the theory and auxiliary problem, Lakatos introduces two additional criteria that must be met before a theory may be rejected. First, "there must exist a rival research program that is powerful enough to account for all the facts of the former program." Second, and more importantly, "the rival research program must anticipate new 'facts,' some of which have been corroborated." (Serlin & Lapsley, p. 77) According to Serlin and Lapsley, these two additional criteria serve to block a number of Meehl's claims. For instance, since, as Serlin and Lapsley (p. 77) claim, there "can be no 'refutation' until the emergence of a more powerful theory," and "the Lakatosian view pits theories against each other," it makes sense to count noses to see who is winning.

The theory and auxiliary problem and the two additional criteria of sophisticated falsification needed to overcome them allow Serlin and Lapsley to defuse the apparent difficulty posed by the slow progress of soft psychology. They conclude:

"Scientific theories are tenacious. They are developed in the face of recalcitrant evidence by the force of suggestion of methodological directives--the heuristic machinery--and are fortified by networks of auxiliary theories. Hence, deliberate progress in psychology [and the allied social sciences] is to be expected, and the seeming reluctance to overthrow a theory faced with recalcitrant facts does not call into question the rational character of psychological research" (Serlin & Lapsley, p. 79). Slow progress is to be expected in complex cases like soft psychology and the social sciences precisely because there are so many more auxiliaries to wade through before a theory can be concisely refuted or declared victorious in competition with other complex theories.

Serlin and Lapsley next turn their attention to the problem posed by the methodological asymmetry between physics and psychology and the apparently "quasi-always false" null hypothesis. We will discuss their solution to this problem in greater detail later. For now a general outline should suffice. The basic idea is to borrow a technique that is typically used in the "hard" sciences, that is, to establish a "good-enough belt" around the expected value of some particular variable . The acceptable difference between the theoretical outcome and the experimental outcome is shown as . Therefore, Serlin and Lapsley recommend that rather than stating the null hypothesis as , we ought to state it as
This difference between the group means is what Serlin and Lapsley call a "good-enough belt." That is, there is always going to be a difference between groups given infinite precision and/or a large sample size (the "always false principle"), but we can control for this condition by deciding beforehand what we would accept as the difference that is truly due to the experimental conditions (i.e., specifications of based on the psychometric error).

Serlin and Lapsley (1985) continue their defense of this sort of hypothesis testing by requiring researchers to decide beforehand on the theoretical direction of the difference. By using the good-enough belt in conjunction with the predetermined directionality, Serling and Lapsley suggest that we would have a methodology that employs the directional null hypothesis and which nearly equals the power of the methodology of the hard sciences. This would make our null hypothesis either

rather than just the "good-enough belt,"
According to Serlin and Lapsley, either of these two
types (directionality or the good enough belt) of null
hypotheses yield two positive results; (1) it allows
for the specification of what would be accepted as
fact: and (2) it allows for a point prediction.

Dar's Point of View

Dar (1987) accepts Serlin and Lapsley's solution
to the "quasi-always false" null hypothesis, but he
rejects their attempt to defer to Kakatos'
sophisticated methodological falsificationism on the
grounds that Lakatos supports Meehl's (1978) critique
and cites several examples of Lakatos' contempt for
psychology. Lakatos (1978a) characterized the
nomological network of psychology as a "patched up,
unimaginative series of pedestrian empirical
adjustments" (p. 88). Further, the net result of
research in the social sciences is "nothing but an
increase in pseudo-intellectual garbage" (p. 88). Dar
(1987) finds Serlin and Lapsley's (1985) appeal to
Lakatos' philosophy of science to be ludicrous given
Lakatos' contempt for social science's attempts at
being scientific. Dar's reaction to Serlin and
Lapsley's paper has 4 major points; (1) the process of
"nose counting" in theory evaluation; (2) ad hoc
explanations of experimental outcomes; (3) appeals to
the ceteris paribus and auxiliary hypotheses; and (4)
null hypothesis testing.

First, recall that Meehl (1978) notes that "nose
counting" in the evaluation of a theory is wrong on the
basis of the logical force of modus tollens. Serlin
and Lapsley's (1985) attempt to appeal to Lakatos to
thwart this argument is, in return, thwarted by Dar
(1987) when he says,

> ...Lakatos' philosophy gives a
> particular science the license to
> be liberal in dealing with
> anomalies and in allowing theories
> to continue to exist in the face of
> experimental refutations, it
> assumes that that science is
> demanding in terms of theory
> building and testing. I suggest
> that Lakatos' expressed disdain for
> psychology and other sciences...
> stems from his belief that these

> sciences do not make much demands
> on theories. (p. 147)

What Dar is emphasizing here, is that "strong" theories need to be built in the social sciences and these theories need then to be vigorously tested. Once these conditions are met, an appeal to Lakatos might seem more defensible.

The second point Dar makes is that the weak theories of soft psychology (and most of the social sciences for that matter), in conjunction with the weakness of null hypothesis testing, means that there will be available some <u>ad hoc</u> explanation regardless of the experimental outcome of some test of a theory. By the weakness of theory in soft psychology, Dar means the loose structure of the nomological network, the loose connection between theory and instrumentation and the inability to make point predictive. This looseness in conjunction with the quasi-always false null hypothesis implies that "<u>either</u> success <u>or</u> failure in a psychological experiment can be accounted for a variety of improvised <u>ad hoc</u> explanation" (p. 147, Author's italics). So regardless of the statistical result of the experiment, there are multiple explanations for the result. This means that there will be no shortage of ways for a clever researcher to defend the logical core of his pet theory (see also, Anderson's 1976 discussion of the "non-identifiability" problem).

Third, Dar (1987) raises the point concerning the relative (to the hard sciences) looseness of auxiliary hypotheses to the theoretical core. This is a very important point because Lakatos' philosophy protects the core theoretical construct from refutation, because direct experimentation is done only on the auxiliary hypotheses and not on the theoretical hard core. In the hard sciences, however, there is an "intimate" relation (often one of derivability) between the auxiliaries and the core theoretical construct, which means that the experiments indirectly affect the theoretical core. In the social sciences, on the other hand, this intimate connection does not exist and "...<u>ad hoc</u> challenges to the auxiliary hypotheses are often little more than afterthoughts that do not have any real consequences for the substantive theory" (Dar, 1987, p. 149).

Dar's final point deals with the problem of null hypothesis testing. He derives three problems with null hypothesis testing from Meehl (1978) and Lakatos (1978a); (1) that the research emphasis in the social sciences is on statistical significance; (2) that statistical significance automatically implies semantic significance or meaningfulness; and (3) that combining powerful statistical techniques with computer technology's accuracy gives the social sciences some credence of scientific respectability.

The first problem with null hypothesis testing Dar (1987) states rather succinctly: "instead of demanding a high level of logical consistency, explanatory power, and accurate predictions from their theories, psychology researchers are trained to feel satisfied when a relevant statistic...is statistically different from zero at the .05 level" (p. 149). Again, he emphasizes the importance of theory building--a practice not well developed in the social sciences. He goes on to point out that graduate programs tend, also, to emphasize sophisticated methods, while not emphasizing at the same time (and it is probably more important) the process of developing good predictive theories. With good theories, statistical significance is unnecessary.

The second problem inherent in null hypothesis testing and the slow progress in psychology is the fact that many social scientists believe (implicitly or explicitly) that a statistically significant result implies a direct correspondence between theory or research hypothesis and reality. This parallels the portion of Meehl's (1978) title that, "Tabular Asterisks" are the goals of social science research. The point both Meehl (in his title) and Dar are making is the fact that a .001 significance level generally creates a great deal of enthusiasm, whether or not the tested theory is meaningful. Statistical significance need not imply semantical significance (meaningfulness) -- much less truth.

The final point Dar raises with regard to null hypothesis testing concerns the reliance on the computer and powerful statistical packages to make our experiments more precise. However, the computer may be the worst thing to ever happen to the social sciences. Researchers tend to make multiple "runs" on their data to get the best results, rather than developing strong theoretical predictions and testing these predictions with the statistics. Perhaps hand calculations should be reintroduced to save the social sciences from data driven theories.

Dar (1987) does not, however, criticize psychological methodology without stating any resolutions to the problems he raises. First, he is impressed with Serlin and Lapsley's solution to the "always false" null hypothesis (with the caveat that one has actually used it). What Dar recommends, as is apparent from the above discussion, is the development of strong theories, which would imply strong research programs. With strong research programs, good predictions can be made and the use of Serlin and Lapsley's modified null hypothesis (can be specified in advance) can be utilized. In addition, he reminds us that Lakatos recommends the practice of replication, a practice not widely followed in the social sciences.

Is the "good-enough" principle good enough?

As indicated, Dar (1987) seems quite satisfied with Serlin and Lapsley's (1985) "good-enough principle." Because we, for our part, are somewhat less comfortable with this notion, we would like to express our concerns before this way of thinking is operationalized and set in methodological concrete. Too facile an acceptance of this principle could well be a serious block to theoretical progress in educational research. Our objections may not be insurmountable, but we feel that they are certainly deserving of careful consideration on the part of educational researchers.

We fear that the "good-enough" principle may be conceived in sin. The sin lies in confusing the substantive theory of interest with the statistical hypothesis that is, or at least ought to be, derived from it. Meehl (1967) warns that "while no competent psychologist is unaware of this obvious distinction between a substantive theory (T) and a statistical hypothesis (H) implied by it in practice there is a tendency to conflate the substantive theory with the statistical hypothesis..." (p. 107) Serlin and Lapsley may well have fallen victim to a more abstract and general case of this conflation and, as a result, their derivation of the good enough principle is confused. In fact we suspect that they have, at least in some places, confused inferential statistical theory with substantive psychological theory. In any event, serious equivocations seem to exist in several places.

Serlin and Lapsley's (1985) derivation of the good enough principle for the point-null case is highly elliptical and it is in trying to fill in the ellipsis that the equivocations and confusions become evident. The passage of interest begins: "A psychologist in the test of an alternative hypothesis of interest, makes the null prediction that a treatment will have zero effect. Hence, the null hypothesis states that a particular variable,   , possesses a certain expected value, which is   ). But because no theory is absolutely true, the value of   can never be exactly equal to the theoretical value, 0" (p. 79).

Let us begin by noting the difficulty in determining the character of   . When it is first introduced,   appears to be a "particular variable," presumably a variable in the investigator's substantive theory. Yet when we see   again it seems to resemble a statistical difference of means
The former use of   is consonant with substantive theory whereas the latter is clearly a statistical hypothesis--an instance of the conflation? At best, Serlin and Lapsley need to make themselves clearer here. That we are confronted with an instance of the conflation seems to follow immediately from the clause that reads "the theoretical value, 0." The statistical null hypothesis,   , certainly is not a <u>value</u> derived from some substantive theory. Indeed, one may well wonder what Serlin and Lapsley mean by "theory."

We are very concerned with the passage that reads "because no theory is absolutely true...." Why not? It is not obvious that there is anything inherent in the activity of theory building that forbids a theory being absolutely true. In fact, we wonder what less than "absolute" truth might be; by the law of excluded middle, something either is true or it isn't. Truth doesn't seem to admit of degrees, at least for a realist. This dubious passage is tantamount to a tacit rejection of theoretical realism. Certainly there are other positions regarding the ontological status of theories; indeed, at least one of the present authors rejects realism as nonsensical. Nevertheless, it does not seem desirable to have one's metaphysics dictated by mere methodological convenience.

Serlin and Lapsley's theoretical anti-realism is not a mere slip of the pen. They require this premise if they are to show that although "the asymmetry between psychology and physics is indeed real enough, it is only real in the sense that the point values tested under the null hypothesis are different" (1985, p. 80). Serlin and Lapsley (1985) write: "But nature is just unkind to physicists as it is to psychologists, in that the true value will never be exactly equal to the theoretical value" (pp. 79-80). In physics, the point prediction is a real point <u>derived</u> from the theory. For the physicist who is a <u>realist</u> about his or her theory, the theoretical point <u>is</u> the true point. If a physicist is a theoretical real<u>ist</u>, as was Albert Einstein for example, then the experimental point prediction, if validity derived from theoretical concepts, <u>is</u> the true value and therefore will never be refuted regardless of the infinite precision of the measuring instruments or the sample size. Serlin and Lapsley attempt to gloss over the problems of asymmetry by saying that the nature of the point values under the null hypothesis is different; but that difference is everything. Physics, to repeat Meehl's argument, <u>derives</u> a physical point prediction or hypothesis from a substantive theory whereas the point-null hypothesis is not derived from anything; it is merely a methodological tool and the predicted point is a methodological not a theoretical point. By taking an antirealist view of theories, Serlin and Lapsley blur the distinction between substantive theory and statistical hypothesis but they cannot erase it. Let us quickly add that an instrumentalist view of theories would not significantly alter any of our foregoing remarks since it too would have no impact on the distinction. We will return to discuss the asymmetry problem further, but first let us see what the rest of Serlin and Lapsley's derivation looks like.

Since "the value of can never be exactly equal to the theoretical value, 0," Serlin and Lapsley continue, "a good-enough belt of width must also be included in the prediction, so that a value of 0 + is predicted. The value of is chosen in advance and reflects the state of the art or the error in the best 'known experimental technique' in the field. When the experiment is performed, a statistical test is applied to determine if is in the range of 0 + . If the data indicate that seems to be in the good-enough belt, then the complex null hypothesis cannot be rejected" (p. 79). Mathematically (and assuming implies a difference of means) this would be written , the point null hypothesis for the "good-enough belt." Again, referring to the above explanation, Serlin and Lapsley use the wording outside the range 0 + " (p. 79) in reference to the alternative hypothesis. The mathematical representation of the alternative hypothesis would, of course, be . Fine, but two pages later Serlin and Lapsley give their mathematically represented null hypothesis as follows: "The null hypothesis must state " (p. 81). This is the exact mathematical opposite of their original derivation of the "good-enough principle."

How things got around we are not sure. Perhaps there was a breakdown in communication as the pen passed from one author's hand to the others. The second version is certainly convenient since it makes hypothesis testing in psychology and the allied social sciences symmetric with the case in physics and would indeed convey the logical impact of modus tollens refutation into the interior of a theory. The difference between the symbol "$\leq$" and "$\geq$" is the asymmetry in a nutshell and under no circumstances, save one, can they be reversed. Here's what happened. In the second case the value is a theoretically derived (mean) point prediction whose value would be zero only by coincidence. Indeed, in their example Serlin and Lapsley use (p. 82). This value is selected arbitrarily, but it is used as if it were a theoretically derived point prediction. When psychology makes a theoretically derived point value prediction it does indeed behave just like the theoretical sciences. Indeed, this is precisely what the difference between soft and hard psychology amount to. Only by blurring yet another distinction can Serlin and Lapsley turn things around like they do. This shift is signalled by the shift in our notation from to . One might say that the difference between hard psychology, for example, and soft psychology is precisely which notation they are able to use, but then that was what puzzled Meehl to begin with. Where are the theories that make precise point predictions in soft psychology in the first place? Let us return to the original derivation of the "good-enough belt."

Serlin and Lapsley want to claim that both psychology and physics "require the methodological decision to employ good-enough belts around parameters under the test to avoid the paradoxical conclusions made inevitable by the prospect of infinite precision" (p. 80). The assumption is that infinite precision in physics must result in refutation just as it does in soft psychology unless we add a "good-enough belt."

This way of thinking seems confused. The notion of a researcher choosing   in advance reverses the practice in physics. In physics the value of   is not determined by the researcher at all; rather it is the result of experimental measurement (not experimental technique) and expresses the lack of precision in the instruments used to carry out the measurements. It is the instruments that carry out the actual measurements that choose, or rather determine, the value of   and not the researcher at all. Once again Serlin and Lapsley succeed in making soft psychology resemble physics by equivocating, only this time by equivocating on   . So before going on, let us distinguish the "good-enough principle" in soft psychology (let us call it   ) from the "good enough belt" in physics (let us call it   ). The two are constructed in an entirely different manner and are in fact as different as an apple is from an orange both of which only happen to be round. We will return to the problem of the reversed construction of   in a moment, but first let us quickly register three relatively minor criticisms en passant.

First, as we pointed out just now, it is the instruments not the research that determines   . Meehl (1978, p. 808) explicitly includes problems in determining a psychometric "unit of measurement" among his 20 difficulties peculiar to the social sciences. Also Meehl writes that in psychology (as compared to physics) "independent testing of the auxiliary theories...often means validation of psychometric instruments...[and] is harder to carry out...[because of the] unavoidable looseness of the nomological network" (Meehl, 1978, see also Cronbach & Meehl, 1955, 1976). Compare this looseness between theory and instrumentation claimed by Meehl to the following description of the same situation provided by the famous physicist and philosopher of science, Pierre Duhem:

>...in the mind of the physicist there are constantly present two sorts of apparatus; one is the concrete apparatus in glass and metal manipulated by him [or her], the other is the schematic and abstract apparatus which theory substitutes for the concrete

apparatus and on which the physicist does his [or her] reasoning, both of these ideas are indissolably connected...each necessarily calls on the other. (Duhem, 1906, 1974, p. 182).

It is hard to imagine the instruments and theory of soft psychology and the allied social sciences mirroring each other in this way.

Second, Serlin and Lapsley (1985) tell us that the value of chosen in advance "reflects the state of the art or error in the best 'known experimental technique' in the field" (p. 79). What we are not told is how it reflects the state of the art. Their edict commands our compliance yet fails to council us in its use. Must we become experimental aestheticians? There exists a theory of error for building in physics (see for example, Beers 1953, 1957); one looks in vain for such a theory of error in Serlin and Lapsley. Without such a theory, amounts to little more than a guess. Trial and error is not good scientific method. Where is the theory of error that permits to be objectively constructed on the bases of instrumental error, or what we commonly call the standard error of measurement. At best Serlin and Lapsley have a large task before them if they are to show a theory of how may be constructed in advance.

Our third concern may appear very minor -- we aren't sure. In any case, we offer it for your consideration. Meehl (1978, p. 825) notes that in physics it is often the case that, rather than a point prediction, a theory may instead entail "a certain function form such as a graph should be an ogive or that it should have three peaks and that these peaks should be increasingly high...." Should experimentation produce such a function form it would be considered a strong corroboration whatever the magnitude of . However inaccurate the measurement, one could almost not help but be impressed that mere theory could predict the shape of anything in empirical nature. It seems to us that the social sciences can also yield function forms, but if so the good-enough principle will offer no help regarding null hypothesis that may depend upon them. Let us now return to the problems offered by the backward construction of

As indicated earlier, the idea of the psychological researcher being able to choose the value of in advance entirely reverses the case in physics. In physics is determined by the precision of the instruments and is always ex post facto. Serlin and Lapsley want us to believe that their is substantially the same as the in physics, but the "topsyturvy" character of their construction betrays them. We suspect that it is necessary to build backwards in order to back into the asymmetry between physics and soft psychology so as to make things appear symmetric enough. Serlin and Lapsley are eager to convince us that infinite precision in physics without a "good-enough belt" would always result in refutation just as it would in soft psychology. They conclude that "both disciplines require the methodological decision to employ good-enough belts around parameters under test to avoid the paradoxical conclusions made inevitable by the prospect of infinite precision (p. 80)." Surely this cannot be correct, especially if the parameter under test is the valid consequence of an absolutely true theory. Let us see what happens to and as we begin to move closer and closer in infinite precision.

Read straightforwardly, it is obvious that as shrinks, that is, as our measuring instruments become more precise, the theoretical point prediction becomes increasingly exposed to refutation. Indeed, only a true theoretical value could survive a perfectly precise ideal measurement. A shrinking only makes H easier to reject, and since there is no theory of error for it is not clear what if any effect enhanced experimental technique will have on it.

Let us see what happens to and in the case of infinite precision. We are told that is chosen on the basis of the "best known experimental technique." Further, given infinite precision, Serlin and Lapsley claim that the "good-enough principle" prevents a "quasi-always false" null hypothesis. However, if we have an infinitely precise measure of psychological parameter, closes to 0, 0 ± closes to 0 ± 0, thereby yielding our old friend the "quasi-always false" null hypothesis. On the other hand, as already indicated, as closes to 0 only an absolutely true theoretical point prediction could avoid refutation. One unhappy result of the asymmetric effect of infinite precision is that any improvement in instrumentation and instrumental precision will increase the likelihood of supporting the theory in soft psychology and the allied social sciences while increasing the probability of disconfirming the theory in physics. Another instance of Meehl's paradox.

There are two things remaining that bother us. We are not sure just how important they may be, but we would like to at least mention them. First there is this: it seems to us that the notion of choosing in advance is not too unlike choosing a prior probability based on one's best theoretical guess. It seems to us that Serlin and Lapsley may be falling into Bayesian statistics. If so, then why bother with null hypothesis predictions at all?

Our second worry occurs at the intersection to theory, metaphysics, epistemology and methodology and may well be the most serious of all. We will pose it as a challenge. Try formulating a statement of Type I or Type II error that does not at least tacitly assume some form of realism. That is, try formulating these two types of error without saying something about the way the world really is. Now we don't want to confuse theoretical and metaphysical realism, if they are in fact distant. Nevertheless, Serlin and Lapsley's solution to Meehl's paradox seems at least on the surface, seriously incompatible with an important internal component of null hypothesis testing.

Conclusion

The purpose of this paper has been to familiarize educational researchers with a debate that has important implications for our field. If Meehl is correct, an immense amount of educational research is wrong headed from the very beginning. Dar effectively refutes Serlin and Lapsley's appeal to Lakatos and if there is anything to our criticism of the construction of then their solution to the problem of the asymmetry between psychology and physics is inadequate or at least, needs a great deal of work. The debate must remain open and the conversation should continue because the issues are simply too important to be ignored. One final comment. The set of three articles reviewed in this paper reflect an ongoing debate in psychology. We have continually put the debate into the context of the allied social sciences. The reason for this is that the field of education borrows many of its theories and methods from other disciplines, not the least of which is psychology. If there are fundamental problems in many areas of psychology, the impact on the field of education is that much greater. Perhaps on this occasion we should not wait passively for the pot to boil over into education.

FOOTNOTES

1. One is inclined to accept the first part of this statement, but Meehl's "20 features that make human psychology hard to scientize" makes us pause. Meehl (1978, pp. 808-817) lists 20 different problems that are inherent in social science research including among other things "unit of measurement," "Sheer Number of Variables" and "Intentionality." Perhaps we should distinguish between the hard sciences like physics and chemistry and the really difficult sciences like psychology and sociology.

2. Albert Einstein was indeed a theoretical realist. When asked by his student, Ilse Rosenthal-Schneider, for his response to the possibility that Eddington's measurements might have turned out incompatible with the predictions of the theory of relativity, Einstein is reported to have said: "Then I would have been sorry for the dear Lord--the theory is correct" (in Clark, 1971, p. 230, see also Rosenthal-Schneider, 1980).

3. Of course there are theories of measurement error that could be used, but Serlin & Lapsley's (1985, p. 82) use of the sample variance multiplied by .5 clearly does not use an error of measurement (e.g., the standard deviation of the error variance in "classical" test theory) nor is any guidance provided for estimating the constant (in this case 0.5 is "given").

REFERENCES

Anderson, J. R. (1976) Language, memory and thought. Hillsdale, N.J.: Lawrence Erlbaum Associates.

Beers, Y. (1953, 1957) Introduction to the theory of error. Addison-Wesley Publishing Company, Reading, Massachusetts.

Clark, Ronald W. (1971) Einstein: The life and times. The World Publishing Company, New York.

Cronbach, L. J. & Meehl, P. E. (1973) "Construct validity in psychological tests." in P. E. Meehl, Psychodiagnosis: Selected papers. Minn: University of Minnesota Press, 3-31.

Dar, R. (1987) "Another look at Meehl, Lakatos, and the scientific practices of psychologists" American Psychologist. 42, 145-151.

Duhem, P. (1906, 1974) Aim and structure of physical theory. (P. P. Wiener, Trans.) New York: Atheneum.

Fisher, R. A. (1967) Statistical methods for research workers (13th ed.) Edinbursh, Scotland: Oliver & Boyd.

Garrison, J. W. (1986) "Some principles of postpositivistic philosophy of science," Educational Researcher, 15, (9), 12-18.

Hays, W. L. (1973) Statistics for the social sciences. (2nd ed.) N.Y.: Holt Rinehart and Winston.

Lakatos, I. (1970) "Falsification and the methodology of scientific research programmes." in I. Lakatos & A. Musgrave (Eds.) Criticism and the growth of knowledge. Cambridge University Press: London, 91-196.

Lakatos, I. (1978a) "Falsification and the methodology of scientific research programs." in J. Worral & G. Currie (Eds.) The methodology of scientific research programs: Imre Lakatos Philosophical papers. (Vol. 1). Cambridge, England: Cambridge University Press, 8-101.

Lakatos, I. (1978b) "Popper on demarcation and induction." in J. Worral & G. Currie (Eds.) The methodology of scientific research programs: Imre Lakatos Philosophical papers. (Vol. 1). Cambridge, England: Cambridge University Press, 139-167.

Meehl, P. E. (1967) "Theory-testing in psychology and physics: A methodological paradox." Philosophy of Science. 34, 103-115.

Meehl, P. E. (1978) "Theoretical risks and tabular asterisks: Sir Karl, Sir Ronald, and this slow progress of psychology." Journal of Consulting and Clinical Psychology. 46, 806-834.

Popper, K. R. (1968) *Conjectures and refutations: The growth of scientific knowledge*. N.Y.: Harper Torchbooks.

Rosenthal-Schneider, Ilse (1980) *Reality and scientific truth*. Wayne State University Pres, Detroit.

Serlin, R. C. & Lapsley, D. K. (1985) "Rationality in psychological research: The good-enough principle." *American Psychologist*. $\underline{40}$, 73-83.

ACKNOWLEDGEMENT

We fully acknowledge the permission of the <u>Journal of Research and Development in Education</u> to include this paper in this work.

THEORETIC AND PRAGMATIC JUSTIFICATIONS
FOR COLLABORATIVE RESEARCH

by

Jeffrey Roth
The University of Florida

Any proposal to reconceptualize the relationship between researchers and subjects--from adversaries to collaborators--must begin by considering alternatives to the positivist notion of research. The inappropriateness of utilizing the nomothetic orientation of positivism to guide social scientific inquiry has been argued repeatedly (see, for example, Comstock, 1982; Guba & Lincoln, 1983). Each of the major discriminations of positivism--defining as real only those phenomena amenable to measurement and manipulation, distinguishing sharply between statements of facts and statements of value, formulating covering laws to increase prediction and control of human behavior--has been attacked as unsuitable ideals for governing discourse about the infinitely complex and willful interactions of human beings (Bowers, 1978). One tenet in particular of positivism has been singled out as especially inappropriate by proponents of rival paradigms for social science research. These two other paradigms--the interpretive and the critical (see Bernstein, 1983; Bredo & Feinberg, 1982)--are united in their assault on the positivist conception of truth-as-correspondence.

The ontological position of positivism assumes there is a reality independent of human mind(s); our knowledge of this reality (unchanging, immanent truth) is commensurate with the degree to which our statements approach and match, that is, correspond to this underlying reality. The chief consequence of working within a realist ontology is a strong preoccupation with accurately measuring the extent to which our recording instruments--and ultimately our minds--have captured, as impassively as a mirror, the contours of this reality.

In place of a truth-as-correspondence view, opponents of positivism argue for a truth-as-agreement view (Miller, 1986). In this ontological perspective, reality is mind-dependent; it is a modifiable framework for meaning constructed out of the set of understandings that prevails among any coherent community of language users. The chief consequence of operating within a "consensual" ontology is a necessity to explore how historically situated social actors use language to define and understand one another.

Among the social situations requiring a negotiation of definitions in order to arrive at mutual understanding is the research situation itself. No theoretician today has provided a more complete or more compelling picture of the ideal of symmetrical communication within the researcher-subject relationship than Juergen Habermas (1971, 1973, 1983, 1984). Habermas' theoretical work is central, even though there has been no dearth of calls from field methodologists for increased sharing of research tasks with subjects. Variously termed "participative," "interactive," or "collaborative,: these proposals are marked by appeals for the close involvement of the people being "observed" in generating and validating new knowledge. Several of these appeals will be examined in the second part of this paper. While they contain reasonable and persuasive arguments for including subjects in the genesis and execution of a study, they uniformly fail to provide any theoretical justification for their recommendations. Habermas, on the other hand, has for the last 20 years been dedicated to constructing a comprehensive "logic" for all types of social scientific inquiry, in which the justification of collaboration occupies a crucial conceptual role.

Construing Research as a Hermeneutical Activity

Habermas is heir to a long tradition in German philosophy that insists on the language-drenched nature of the Geisteswissenschaften, the social or human sciences as opposed to the physical or natural sciences (Polkinghorne, 1983). It is not pertinent here to review this tradition that originates with Kant. Suffice it to say that it makes a sharp distinction between the physical and the social sciences: Understanding in the former is achievable through mastery of the logical, artificial language of mathematics whereas understanding in the latter has no other medium save the semantics of ordinary language. Moreover, the objects of study in the natural sciences do not talk; quite the opposite is the case in the social sciences. It is no exaggeration to say that language, specifically how human beings use it to create and communicate meanings, is the prominent object of study as well as the social scientist's chief analytical tool.

The discernment of meaning is what makes the social sciences a hermeneutic activity. Understanding the speech and action of others is a judgment made not only by social scientists but by all people as they carry out the intercourse of daily life. Bringing forth a convergence out of these divergent understandings is a goal of the philosophical tradition within which Habermas works. Habermas has criticized some of his predecessors in this tradition for their latent positivism. He sees in the writings of the Verstehen theorists (such as Dilthey and Weber) a tendency to treat understandings, value systems, and core beliefs as data, in the root sense of something given, as opposed to something contingently constructed out of the rhetorical engagement between speakers belonging to different traditions. In this conception of hermeneutics as a conversation within and across cultures, dialogue occupies a crucially important place in Habermas' logic for the social sciences.

It is through dialogue that the assignment of meaning and intention is accomplished. A dialogic orientation permits the interpretation that is to be affixed to behavior to emerge after an unconstrained exchange of divergent perspectives. For Habermas, the speakers in the hermeneutic conversation are obliged to make clear the bases of their judgments. Habermas makes absolutely clear that the participants in any investigation of social life are engaging in acts of self and mutual definition and are operating from specific sets of interests. Researchers, for example, who claim that disengagement is necessary in order to arrive at unequivocal findings are declaring that they prefer to construct their interpretations monologically.

Habermas (1971) considers the monologic approach flawed. He describes it as an inappropriate application of instrumental reason, by which he means a form of rationality that restricts itself to judging the efficacy of means and excludes discussing the worthwhileness of ends. Instrumental reason is appropriate in some of the physical sciences where the objects of inquiry (e.g., molecules and quasars--as far as we know now, mute entities) do not present justifications. Speakers of natural languages, however, can convey possibilities and alternatives.

In Habermas' (1971) conception of dialogue, the level of understanding to be achieved extends far beyond mutual comprehension. Dialogue is the process by which a rational consensus is constructed. Habermas classifies dialogue as a form of discourse characterized by an exchange of justifications. In the ideal speech situation, all of the speakers are competent and willing to encourage one another to express their motivations and expectations. The bases of their interests are made explicit during a process of negotiation whose ultimate goal is the creation of an unconstrained, genuine, and sincere consensus about the methods and goals of an inquiry. Habermas has continuously revised the dimensions of the ideal speech situation in his writings, but his emphasis on its essential dialogic structure has remained constant. Since I intend to examine the pragmatic justifications for researcher-subject involvement in the light of Habermas' ongoing effort to project a consensual agenda for social scientific inquiry, one that does not merely passively respect subjects but actively empowers them, I need to provide a few more details from his general theory of communicative action (Habermas, 1984).

Dialogue without Domination

Habermas has long been engaged in constructing a comprehensive theory that links certain kinds of communication to certain kinds of outcomes. The particular linkage I want to discuss in this section is the one between discourse and consensus. In Habermas' scheme, discourse does not refer to conversations in which participants exchange information or convey experiences; rather, it is a special rhetorical form of communication used to question and discuss the assumptions underlying speakers' evaluative judgments. Discourse uses language forensically: Justifications are offered by speakers to support their interpretation of an event or practice. Deciding on an interpretation that accurately and fairly represents the interests of all parties requires that the supporting justifications be evaluated through a negotiatory process that judges the cogency of the arguments each speaker advances.

To engage in discourse implies a commitment to the possibility of rationally assessing the merit of different interpretations. For Habermas, it is axiomatic of discursive communication that the forcefulness of a better argument is potentially recognizable by all speakers. "Interpreters can do no other than appeal to standards of rationality which they themselves have adopted as binding on all parties" (Habermas, 1983, p. 259). The interpretation most likely to be ultimately accepted by all speakers is one that succeeds in establishing a commonality among diverse interests. No single viewpoint has a privileged epistemological or ethical status; incorrigibility is not accorded on a priori grounds to accounts by either completely subjective or completely objective speakers.

For discourse to arrive at consensus it must take place in what Habermas calls an "ideal speech" situation. In such a situation the construction of an interpretation agreeable to all speakers rests solely on the persuasive power of forceful argumentation. The situation is termed ideal when the presence of distortive influences are made explicit. Two sources of potential distortion--both external and antecedent to the inquiry--are the speakers' asymmetrical social status and their unacknowledged desire to dominate each other. Habermas has consistently maintained that the relationship between researchers and subjects has strong similarities to the psychotherapeutic relationship: The goal of both is uninhibited and truthful self-expression. (See, for example, "Postscript" in Habermas, 1971.) To take up Habermas' argument that social science is an emancipatory project is beyond my present purpose. Suffice it to say that for Habermas the goal of discursive communication is to arrive at an understanding; and, in his theory, this goal --Verstaendigung--has the very broad sense of "shared knowledge, mutual trust, and accord" (Keat, 1981, p. 181).

How exactly is consensus achieved? It is the product of hermeneutic dialogue: During the course of an inquiry a provisional interpretive scheme is jointly constructed and continuously modified as a result of negotiations that seek to establish an intersubjective understanding among all parties. The basis for intersubjectivity is the constant rotation from speaker to listener, from actor to observer. Alternating between defining and being defined, the participants in the inquiry assess one another's understanding by requesting and giving accounts of events. In telling their story, speakers try to make explicit the values or norms that guide their judgments. This process of negotiating a mutually agreeable interpretation of collective action is predicated on the exchange of justifications, or validity claims, as Habermas terms them. Validity claims (Habermas distinguishes four different kinds) become incorporated into the rational consensus only if all speakers give their consent.

It is of paramount importance to Habermas that consensus be achieved without recourse to any form of coercion. Coercion produces a false consensus; it distorts the rationality of the communicative process. Instead of an account of social life that expresses the generalized interests of all participants, monologically conducted research proffers its own justifications exclusively. The refusal to engage in dialogue results in distorted communication. The unwillingness of researchers, for example, to relinquish the role of disinterested observer obstructs the hermeneutical construction of meaning.

> Understanding requires participation and not merely observation....Interpreters sacrifice the superiority of observers' privileged position, since they are involved in the negotiations about validity claims. By taking part in communicative actions they accept an equal standing with those whose utterances they want to understand. They are no longer immune... but give in to a process of mutual criticism. Within a communicative process, ...there is no a priori decision as to who has to learn from whom in order to reach a common understanding. (Habermas, 1983, pp. 256-57)

Dialogue without domination provides a circumstance within which all speakers can express their motives and intentions openly. Equality among interpreters has two effects. First, it enhances the sense of agency that each group possesses; each group contributes to the story that will be told about what happened when speakers with different "horizons of expectations" met and interacted. Second, the opportunity to participate in the construction of a consensus increases interpreters' awareness of their own individuality. In assessing the plausibility of different interpretations, speakers discover the presence and operation of their own particular set of interests. "Meaning discloses itself to the interpreter only to the extent that his own world becomes clarified at the same time" (Habermas, 1971, p. 309).

It should be clear from the foregoing why Habermas' theory of communicative action is so relevant to a reconceptualization of research as a collaborative activity. First is his insistence that all social inquiry is language-bound, that it involves dialogue between speakers belonging to different cultural traditions who need to come to an agreement about the meanings to be assigned to action. Second is his position that since social inquiry is essentially a hermeneutical enterprise, some method for pooling interpretations is necessary. Third is his assertion that a consensus about meaning can only come about in unconstrained circumstances where the contributions of all speakers possess equal validity.

Habermas' views are important because he vigorously disputes the positivist claim that monologically constructed, rigorously neutral accounts of social processes can be valid. On the contrary, he warns that such accounts, which fail to establish a consensus of meaning acceptable to all participants, are epistemologically and ethically flawed. In fact, by performing the work of analysis and synthesis in isolation, researchers actually impede the exercise of intelligence and autonomy that the informed consent agreement at least in spirit is supposed to encourage. It is time now to consider some recent appeals to include subjects in the course of research.

Collaboration: The Search for Specific Reciprocal Benefits

In this section I want to demonstrate how Habermas' model of communicative action can be used to support an interpretation of informed consent as an agreement between subjects and researchers to enter into and maintain a conversation. I begin by recalling the objections of field methodologists to the required announcing of "risk" factors in "harmless" observational studies. Because they consider naturalistic observation far less intrusive than controlled experimentation, field methodologists insist that researchers have virtually nothing to warn subjects about; in fact, because they are there to learn, rather than prove something, they actually have very little information to communicate in advance. Therefore, instead of a forecast of possible long range risks and benefits, they suggest that the form of antecedent notification more appropriate to social research is the quid pro quo.

> Informed consent may not be so much at issue as establishing clearly understood reciprocity agreements. (Keith-Spiegel & Koocher, 1985, p. 407)

> Emergent reciprocal benefit, not informed consent, has to be the moral basis of fieldwork. (Wax, 1982, p. 38)

The conceptual portion of the field methods literature recognizes that human actors are concerned with the judgments that observers attach to their social performance; therefore, arrangements for doing research have to take into account this tendency to try and shape the opinion of onlookers.

> The ideal model for the conduct of social research investigators--sometimes referred to as the participatory model--is one in which subjects and investigators are seen as equal partners in a mutually advantageous effort. It is a model that emphasizes the rights of respondents in decision making before and during the research process and that deemphasizes status differences between researcher and researched and that accentuates the application of general societal norms of interpersonal relations to the procedures of research. (Bower & de Gasparis, 1978, p. 64)

This formulation is important because it places research very definitely in the category of a communicative transaction, a categorization that implies that there is no basis for exempting research from the function of communicative transaction, which is to generate intersubjective understanding. Bower and de Gasparis (1978) concede, however, that they are describing an ideal form of research: "Equal status participation still remains as a goal for the conduct of research, even though not fully achieved in practice" (p. 64). While there continue to be few instances of full-fledged collaboration with subjects in published field studies, the effect of adopting the participatory model makes it incumbent on researchers to be as explicit as possible with subjects as to what exactly is going to be exchanged.

An Exchange of Meanings

Fieldworkers often continue to portray themselves in the guise of 19th century naturalists. Roaming through but scarcely disturbing strange habitats, they carefully obtain, remove, and carry back specimens to their study. Instead of noting differences in finch beaks and tortoise shells, ethologists of homo socialist examine samples of language and gesture, on the basis of which they assign subspecies to different niches in particular ecosystems. (Proponents of qualitative techniques in program evaluation are especially fond of the idea of collecting definitions. See, for example, MacDonald, 1976, and Patton, 1982.) However, the recent legislation making informed consent procedures mandatory secures the possibility that the occupants of the niches may at any time exercise the right to contest a structural description (i.e., an interpretation) of their ecosystem with which they do not agree.

> Individuals and groups must resist research that could provide an interpretation of the situation different from their own....These groups want to participate in the research itself so that the findings remain in the community's history and discourse. (Rist, 1981, pp. 271-2)

Once the right of individuals and groups to define themselves is recognized, it becomes apparent that the researcher's definition of a social practice is one among several; the views of all participants in a studied situation are the product of their constitutive interests. Habermas' hermeneutical approach to communicative action makes it clear that the researcher's task doesn't consist of adjudicating whose set of definitions most closely approximates the propositional contents of some particular theory of social organization. Rather, the social scientist's project is to promote a continuous exchange of interpretations about the studied situation until one evolves which contains a consensus, not only about what has gone on but also about what should go on. Agreeing on meaning is preliminary to agreeing on future action. The purpose of engaging in dialogue is to redirect practice. Therefore, hermeneutically oriented research is never merely taxonomic as much research in the physical sciences is; it is inescapably normative.

An Exchange of Knowledge

The exchange of interpretations is not simply one in which subjects and researchers alternately present decontextualized definitions of their own and one another's behavior. The hermeneutic dialogue has to be rooted in the specifics of the situation being studied. One way to describe the exchange is to say that each party contributes a different kind of expertise to the conversation. Kyle and McCutcheon (1985, p. 174), for example, use the dichotomy of practitioner craft knowledge vis-a-vis researcher theory building. This is variant of the controversial emic/etic duality, which, according to some writers on the theory of research (e.g., Harris, 1979) is actually a barrier to creating an understanding between speakers who employ different communicative systems. To characterize the exchange on the basis of an insider/outsider, concrete/abstract duality has two problems: It implies that subjects act without reference to any general theory of action, a claim that Giddens (1977), among others, says is blatantly false, since without algorithms no novel responses would ever be generated; it also suggests that researchers' chief purpose in conducting empirical research is to refine the explanatory theorems of their disciplines (see, e.g., Jarvie, 1983.)

Kyle and McCutcheon's delineation of two different kinds of expertise is not wholly conceptual, however. They do share Rist's (1981) more factual version of the quid pro quo. According to Rist, the academic training and field experience of researchers enable them to bring to a site knowledge of how a similar problem was addressed elsewhere by a different group of actors. Only to the extent that all participants see the relevance and utility of the solutions tried elsewhere can researchers' knowledge of past and current procedures be considered a contribution to dialogue. Scriven (1986) argues that those people in the setting already familiar with its practical problems are the best source for establishing the parameters of an investigation. The research questions originate with their expressed concerns, not in the diffuse, transitory curiosity of the visitor.

> [Researchers]have to work on problems whose importance is clear to someone beside themselves (p. 54)

> [Practitioners'] 'knowing how' can serve as the basis for [researchers'] 'knowing that.' (p. 59)

A Sharing of Duties

Consensus emerges not just from sharing meanings but from sharing duties. Collaboration, in fact, supplies a test of the extent to which an agreement about the conceptual framework extends into the realm of action. Increasingly, also, collaboration is a requirement for funded research. Since 1980, for example, one of the criteria used by the National Institute of Education for evaluating research proposals is "evidence that, where appropriate, there is collaboration between investigator and practitioner in defining research questions and conducting research" (cited by Kyle & McCutcheon, 1984, p. 173).

Most writers who have proposed models for collaborative research (e.g., Mehan, 1979; Tikunoff & Ward, 1980; Walker & Wiedel, 1985) conceive of it as a conjoint activity, not a division of labor. At each stage of the inquiry--from proposal to publication-- decisions about means and ends are arrived at jointly. The participation of all parties in the collection, analysis, and dissemination of data is presented as the ideal arrangement. The reason there are so few instances of this deal in practice is that, as Habermas' theory predicts, there most certainly will be very discrepant views about the warrants for each of these activities. Differing justifications will be presented, at least initially, by means of insincere and distorted communication, as various speakers disguise their true interests. For genuine collaboration to occur, dialogue has to be continuous. At each stage of the project, the various speakers need to exchange their interpretations of one anothers' actions. In the process of contrasting intentions, the underlying ethical and epistemological assumptions of each set of speakers come to light. Continuous discussion about the direction and purpose of the inquiry makes prominent where lines of commonality intersect.

One area in the sharing of duties is absolutely crucial for producing a kind of research outcome that has meaning and utily for all participants: Writing up the account of the study has to be a joint responsibility. Without involvement in the final report, subjects risk having their problematic situation reduced to a piece of evidence supporting the researcher's refinement of a current theory. Few writers give much attention to the writing stage, though it is perhaps the most important part of the articulation process. An exception is Desforges et al. (1986) who write that "projects which absolve participants of writing run the risk of absolving them from thinking" (p. 72).

Advantages of Collaboration

Benefit to Subjects

That the invitation to include subjects in the research process may not be a response to the principles of human dignity and empowerment implied by informed consent legislation but rather may simply be another, subtle strategy for reducing reactive behavior has not escaped the notice of some research methodologists.

> Is the game of reciprocity through which we maintain our relations in the field just another technique, another strategy for getting close to the data? (MacDonald & Norris, 1981, p. 285)

Others, for example Gottdiener (1979) and Tikunoff and Ward (1980), take a less skeptical, more _positive_ position with regard to the virtues of enlisting subjects in assembling the research product. Patton (1982), speaking of Tikunoff and Ward's (1980) call for interactive research, says that the "meaningfulness" of a report's findings will be increased "because [subject] participation makes the research less intrusive, reducing rather than increasing reactivity" (pp. 215-216).

Whether one considers the opportunity for collaboration a disguise masking ever more subtle levels of manipulation or a route to a more comprehensive representation of reality (for a statement of the latter position, see Light & Kleiber, 1981), it does seem logical that when subjects are involved in the investigation of interaction, their sense of being treated as an object might lessen. Yet there is a paradox to subjecting behavior to analysis. The opportunity to observe and comment on one's own behavior cuts two ways: It can produce as strong a sensation of being a non-volitional object as when one is objectified by the gaze of others. It can also reveal one's impact and influence on the dynamics of a group, thus vivifying the sense of agency. Suffice it to say here that collaboration may close the door on one form of reactivity--resistance to being objectified by others--and open the door onto another--uncertainty about the extent of one's agency.

Another virtue usually accorded collaborative research (e.g., Cassell, 1982a; Sieber, 1982; Wax, 1980) is that in the course of the project subjects acquire the experience and expertise to conduct additional investigations of their practice long after researchers have departed for other sites. Leaving behind the conceptual apparatus for further self-examination is likely to be, according to Elden (1985), more important even than the generation of the original, jointly-produced report. This vision of seeding research skills is especially attractive to methodologists such as Elden and Walker (1980) who defend small-scale research projects in industrial and educational settings. Disappointment with contradictory findings from expensive, large-scale social research projects has made the intensive case study approach an attractive alternative.

Walker (1980) envisions practitioners at different sites exchanging reports about their experiences in implementing change. He acknowledges that practitioners always trade concrete information about what works--usually through informal channels, sometimes in formal settings. The purpose for the initial collaboration with professional researchers is to organize pieces of craft knowledge into conceptual categories. By abstracting current practices to form a local--in contrast to a grand or midrange--theory, a process that Elden (1985) calls "articulating pretheoretical knowledge" (p. 264), practitioners are then in a position to discuss and evaluate proposed new procedures on the basis of the extent to which they facilitate or impede the goals implied by their theory.

Benefit to Researchers

Collaboration has the effect of enlarging the area in which the interests of researchers and subjects overlap. If subjects also adopt a questioning outlook toward their quotidian transactions, do researchers have to modify their role of solitary observer, scrutinizing from the periphery? Perhaps the most immediate benefit of sharing responsibilities will be a simple diminution of the researcher's workload. Since most investigations of everyday life are labor-intensive, any assistance in conducting interviews, thematizing fieldnotes, or drafting preliminary reports would be welcome, particularly from people who have a stake in the recommendations that eventually are to be put forward.

The reader may well ask, does the presence of more "hands on board" free researchers to instruct people unfamiliar with techniques of data collection and analysis? The answer to his question involves extending the conception of the researcher's role to include direct pedagogy. Providing subjects with occasions for reflecting critically on their actions has to become part of the methodology of research.

> If the fieldworker conceives of knowledge as something that he or she is morally <u>obliged</u> to return, in ways that <u>will</u> enhance the autonomy of those studied, perhaps some of its harmful potential may be neutralized. Feedback, then, rather than being [an optional] part of a personal transaction between researcher and researched, would become part of recognized

> research practice. (Cassell, 1982b, p. 159)

Cassell's point is that the involvement of subjects is not defensible simply as a practical step that enlarges the number of people carrying out the tasks of research; rather the sharing of duties--with sufficient information on how to accomplish them--is a moral obligation for the researcher. When they encourage subjects to exercise their communicative and investigate skills, researchers demonstrate respect for the agency and intelligence of those from whom and about whom they hope to learn. Collaboration is the means by which the prescriptive, inhibitory interpretation of informed consent is transformed to honor its educative potential. Rather than garnering passive cooperation with warnings and promises, researchers can elicit active cooperation when they structure their inquiry as a jointly-conducted search for understanding.

Active engagement by subjects in the research task is not merely an ethical corrective to the covert manipulativeness implicit in the strictly legalistic interpretation of informed consent. There are epistemological payoffs as well: Accuracy as well as fairness can be enhanced. A team approach ensures that more perspectives will be recorded. The more perspectives represented, the stronger is a study's external validity (Woods, 1979, p. 236.) When researchers allow their interpretive frameworks to be revised by debating meaning with subjects, they submit the story that is going to be told to a process of validation. Even positivists, loyal to the correspondence idea of truth, find value in verifying the emerging account with group members.

> The truth of our analyses, their validity, is constituted by establishing some sort of correspondence between an analyst's and collectivity members' view of their social world....One can only establish a correspondence between the sociologist's and the member's view of the member's social world by exploring the extent to which members recognize, give assent to, the judgments of the sociologist. (Bloor, 1978, p. 548)

This positivist formula for securing validity through member checks leaves intact separate spheres for researchers and subjects. It merely adds an additional step to research methodology--soliciting subjects' approval of researchers' account. Habermas' concept of dialogue, however, makes clear that establishing validity is a continuous process, one that begins as soon as any set of speakers advance claims in defense of their actions. Once researchers express their intention to study a social situation, their interpretation of causes and consequences is likely to be contested by speakers whose interpretations emanate from a different set of interests. When the research design encourages a two way communication of interpretations, both the distinctiveness and the commonality in the various speakers' sets of interests become explicit. Where dialogue is authentic and sincere, the partiality of the researcher's position becomes first rationally apparent and then eminently acceptable.

REFERENCES

Bernstein, R. (1983). Beyond objectivism and relativism: Science, hermeneutics and praxis. Philadelphia: University of Pennsylvania Press.

Bloor, M. (1978). On the analysis of observational data: A discussion of the worth and uses of inductive techniques and respondent validation. Sociology, 12, 545-552.

Bower, R. T., & de Gasparis, P. (1989). Ethics in social research: Protecting the interests of human subjects. New York: Praeger.

Bowers, C. A. (1978). Educational critics and technocratic consciousness: Looking into the future through a rear view mirror. Teachers College Record, 80, 272-286.

Bredo, E., & Feinberg, W. (Eds.). (1982). Knowledge and values in social and educational research. Philadelphia: Temple University Press.

Cassell, J. (1982a). Harms, benefits, wrongs, and rights in fieldwork. In J. Sieber (Ed.), The ethics of social research: Vol. 2 Fieldwork, regulation and publication (pp. 7-31). New York: Springer-Verlag.

Cassell, J. (1982b). Does risk-benefit analysis apply to moral evaluation of social research? In T. L. Beauchamp, R. R. Faden, R. J. Wallace, Jr., & L. Walters (Eds.), Ethical issues in social science research (pp. 144-162). Baltimore: Johns Hopkins University Press.

Comstock, D. E. (1982) A method for critical research. In E. Bredo & W. Feinberg (Eds.), Knowledge and values in social and educational research (pp. 370-390). Philadelphia: Temple University Press.

Desforges, C., Cockburn, A., & Bennett, N. (1986). Teachers' perspectives on matching: Implications for action research. In D. Hustler, A. Cassidy, & E. C. Cuff (Eds). Action research in classrooms and schools (pp. 67-72). London: Allen & Unwin.

Elden, M. (1981). Sharing the research work: Participative research and role demands. In P. Reason & J. Rowan (Eds.), Human inquiry: A sourcebook of new paradigm research (pp. 253-266). Chichester, England: John Wiley.

Giddens, A. (1979). Central problems in social theory: Action, structure and contradiction in social analysis. Berkeley: University of California Press.

Gottdiener, M. (1979). Field research and videotape. Sociological Inquiry, 49(4), 59-66.

Guba, E., & Lincoln, Y. S. (1983). Epistemological and methodological bases of naturalistic inquiry. In G. F. Madaus, M. S. Scriven, & D. L. Stufflebeam (Eds.), Evaluation models: Viewpoints on education and human services evaluation (pp. 311-333). Boston: Kluwer-Nijhoff.

Habermas, J. (1971). Knowledge and human interests (J. J. Shapiro, Trans.). Boston: Beacon Press.

Habermas, J. (1973). Theory and practice (J. Viertel, Trans.). Boston: Beacon Press.

Habermas, J. (1983). Interpretive social science vs. hermeneuticism. In H. Haan, R. N. Bellah, P. Rabinow, & W. M. Sullivan (Eds.), Social science as moral inquiry (pp. 251-269). New York: Columbia University Press.

Habermas, J. (1984). The theory of communicative action: Vol. 1. Reasons and the rationalization of society (T. McCarthy, Trans.). Boston: Beacon Press.

Harris, M. (1979). Cultural materialism: The struggle for a science of culture. New York: Random House.

Jarvie, I. C. (1983). The problem of the ethographic real. Current Anthropology, 24, 313-319.

Keat, R. (1981). The politics of social theory: Habermas, Freud and the critique of positivism. Chicago: University of Chicago Press.

Keith-Spiegel, P. & Koocher, G. (1985) Ethics in psychology: Professional standards and cases. New York: Random House.

Kyle, D. W., & McCutcheon, G. (1984). Collaborative research: Development and issues. Journal of Curriculum Studies, 16, 173-179.

Light, L., & Kleiber, N. (1981). Interactive research in a feminist setting: The Vancouver Women's Health Collective. In D. A. Messerschmidt (Ed.), Anthropologists at home in North America: Methods and issues in the study of one's own society (pp. 167-182). Cambridge, England: Cambridge University Press.

MacDonald, B. (1976). Evaluation and the control of education. In D. Tawney (Ed.), Curriculum evaluation today: Trends and implications (pp. 125-136). London: Macmillan.

MacDonald, B., & Norris, N. (1981). Twin political horizons in evaluation fieldwork. In T. S. Popkewitz & B. R. Tabachnick (Eds.), The study of schooling: Field based methodologies in educational research and evaluation (pp. 276-290). New York: Praeger.

Mehan, H. (1979). Learning lessons: Social organization in the classroom. Cambridge, MA: Harvard University Press.

Miller, S. (1986). Some comments on keeping the quantitative-qualitative debate open. Educational Researcher, 15(9), 24-25.

Patton, M. Q. (1982). Practical evaluation. Beverly Hills, CA: Sage.

Rist, R. C. (1981). On what we know (or think we do): Gatekeeping and the social control of knowledge. In T. S. Popkewitz & B. R. Tabachnick (Eds.), The study of schooling: Field based methodologies in educational research and evaluation (pp. 265-272). New York: Praeger.

Scriven, M. (1986) Evaluation as a paradigm for educational research. In E. R. House (Ed.), New directions in educational evaluation (pp. 53-67). London: Falmer Press.

Sieber, J. (1982). Ethnographic fieldwork and beneficial reciprocity. In J. Sieber (Ed.), The ethics of social research: Vol. 2. Fieldwork, regulation, and publication (pp. 1-6). New York: Springer-Verlag.

Tikunoff, W., & Ward, B. (1980). Interactive research and development on teaching. San Francisco: Far West Laboratory for Educational Research and Development.

Walker, R. (1980). The conduct of educational case studies: Ethics, theory and procedures. In W. B. Dockrell & D. Hamilton (Eds.), Rethinking educational research (pp. 30-63). London: Hodder & Stoughton.

Walker, R. & Wiedel, J. (1985). Using photographs in a discipline of words. In R. G. Burgess (Ed.), Field methods in the study of education (pp. 191-216). London: Falmer Press.

Wax, M. L. (1980). Paradoxes of 'consent' to the practice of fieldwork. Social Problems, 27, 272-283.

Wax, M. L. (1982). Research reciprocity instead of informed consent. In J. Sieber (Ed.), The ethics of social research: Vol. 2 Fieldwork, regulation, and publication (pp. 33-48). New York: Springer-Verlag.

Woods, P. (1979). *The divided school*. London: Routledge & Kegan Paul.